A PASSION TO TEACH

Fifty-Eight Years
of Humorous, Weird,
& Engaging Tales

RICHARD V. KOWLES

ISBN 13: 978-0-97788-321-9

Library of Congress Catalog Number: 2013939149

Printed in the United States of America

First Printing: 2013

17 16 15 14 13   5 4 3 2 1

Cover and interior design by James Monroe Design, LLC.

Beaver's Pond Press, Inc.
7108 Ohms Lane
Edina, MN 55439–2129
(952) 829-8818
www.BeaversPondPress.com

To order contact:

Gilmore Creek Press
1293 Country Drive
Winona, MN 55987
Richard V. Kowles
(507) 452-1758

schoolhouse3@charter.net

To all of my teachers
in high school, undergraduate college, and graduate school
who played an important role in the development
of my own long teaching career.

Acknowledgements

Rose Kowles, my life partner, provided input, help, and encouragement throughout this project. Saint Mary's University of Minnesota gave the author permission to use many of the photographs that became part of the book. Laurie Robertson was always willing to give technical help whenever such problems arose. Dara Beevas, Alicia Ester, and Tom Kerber, Beavers Pond Press, were knowledgeable, intuitive, and professional advisors in the overall production of the book. Also, their friendly interaction with the author was still another plus. Jay Monroe of James Monroe Designs and April Michelle Davis of Editorial Inspirations, proved to be instrumental in bringing the book to fruition. A well-deserved acknowledgement needs to be given to the many teachers who inspired the author and the thousands of students who endured him in the classroom. They provided the author with the numerous tales related in this book, and they made his long teaching career interesting and downright fun.

Contents

PART III
FINALLY BECOMING A PROFESSOR

PART IV
PEDAGOGICAL ASPECTS

Part I

THE ROAD TO A
TEACHING CAREER

Chapter 1

Much to Remember

I am a person who has never been able to make an escape from school: six years of grade school, two years of junior high school, four years of high school, four years of undergraduate college (a practice teacher during the senior year), and then two master's degrees and a Ph.D.—all of which led to fourteen years of teaching at the high school level, two years as a teaching assistant while in graduate school, thirty-seven years teaching at the college level, and four years teaching with professor emeritus status. I have taught in high schools on the Minnesota Iron Range, in a southern Minnesota agricultural region, and in a Saint Paul suburb. I have taught in a public college and at a private university. I have taught in a small college and at a major university.

It has been a marvelous career, first as a high school teacher and then as a geneticist/cell biologist in a college setting. Each position was important to me whether it was explaining to middle school students how a lever system works or explaining to a high school biology class how a grasshopper undergoes respiration or explaining to upper-

1

division science students in college how thermodynamics is involved in the living cell. Sometimes I think that genes must exist for the propensity to teach. If so, there is no doubt that I own these genes.

The teaching record amounts to fifty-eight years of enjoyment, comic relief, reward, great satisfaction, and other pleasant emotions. However, the record also shows fifty-eight years of occasional mistakes, near disasters, downright blunders, and other such teacher foibles. Numerous situations have occurred over the fifty-eight years, and I enjoy sharing the stories with others. Some stories are humorous, some have human interest, some are sad, and some are even a bit disgusting.

So what happens during fifty-eight years of academic employment? I taught eighteen different courses that include high school, adult education, college, and graduate school curricula. I showed up for approximately 30,000 classes, 3,500 laboratory sessions, and played a role in the lives of over 10,000 students. I corrected 2,400 sets of examinations, and because it is of the way of science, I read over 30,000 lab reports and advised over 240 undergraduate research theses. I survived over fifty boring faculty workshops, over fifty dull commencements, and an infinite number of tiresome meetings (resulting in many spontaneous naps). However, if you can survive the purgatory of these latter activities, and if you truly love to teach, you suffer zero burnouts.

Over such a long period of time, a teacher can experience technological transformations from blackboards and chalk to whiteboards and black pens; from overhead projectors to 35 mm slides to power point images; from mimeograph machines to Xerox copiers, to computers with printers. I sometimes would indicate to my students that I began teaching by writing on birch bark with a piece of charcoal. In fact, I once began a seminar with birch bark and charcoal. Anything for a laugh!

Often there are rewards and awards, all of which result in a great amount of satisfaction and humility during a teacher's livelihood. Awards shape a teacher's perspective on being part of a wonderful profession that is so appreciative of what we do. At several institutions where I taught, I was fortunate to receive teaching awards. While teaching at the high school level, I was awarded the Teacher of the Year at one of the schools. At Saint Mary's University of Minnesota, I was the recipient of its prestigious University Teaching Award. In 1984, I received the Minnesota Science Teacher of the Year award from the Minnesota Academy of Sciences, and in 1985 Saint Mary's University awarded me the rank of Distinguished University Professor of Biology—only one other person has been given this rank in the history of the university.

Upon semiretirement, the university gave me the rank of Distinguished University Professor Emeritus and also honored me by naming its annual invited lecture for the Undergraduate Research Symposium as the R. V. Kowles Lecture. In addition, Winona State University from which I am an alumnus honored me with the Distinguished Alumnus award and also entered me into its Athletic Hall of Fame. Only one other alumnus in Winona State University's history has ever received both of these awards. I was also awarded the Presidential Medal for Outstanding Merit at Saint Mary's University. A teaching career can indeed be remarkably gratifying.

The content of this book relates to numerous episodes in and out of the classroom. In some cases, personal opinions are given. However, I am not necessarily professing a right or wrong way to teach our young people. I do not regard myself as an expert, and I do not wish to tell others how to do these very important tasks. The book simply offers my personal account of fifty-eight years in the profession, relating my own experiences, my own ideas, my own biases, and my own results.

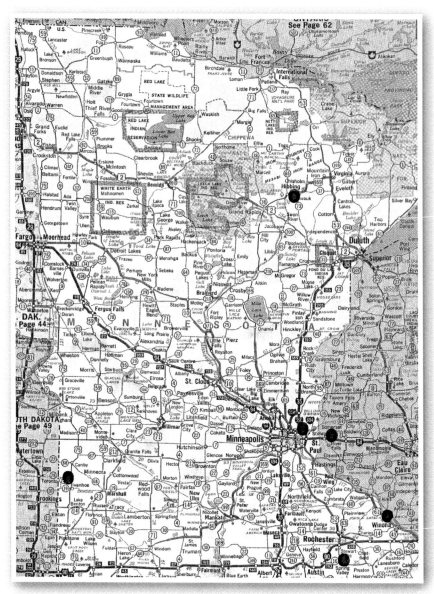

The academic journey of mine leads from Ivanhoe, Minnesota (high school education) to Winona (undergraduate college education) to Keewatin (teaching high school) to Spring Valley (teaching high school) to Mounds View of suburban Saint Paul (teaching high school) to the University of Minnesota in the Twin Cities (Ph.D. degree education) to the University of Wisconsin at River Falls (teaching college) and back to Winona (teaching at Saint Mary's University of Minnesota for forty years).

Chapter 2
Experiencing Good Teachers and the Other Kind

In Winona, Minnesota, located in the southeastern part of the state, a nun was showing us wide-eyed children around during one of the first days of the dreaded first grade. Kindergarten didn't exist in those early days. The event was probably orientation. School was a brand new adventure, and we were all somewhat uncertain about everything. This room was for this, and that room was for that. Nuns in those days all wore apparel called the habit. They all tended to look alike, but I always wondered what the nuns really looked like underneath those penguin suits.

This one nun serving as our tour guide was different in ways well beyond her habit. She had a stern face of stone behind rimless glasses situated low on her rather large nose. I could immediately tell that she really meant business. And she left no doubt about her intentions to scare the heck out of us. Sister "What's Her Name" slowly opened a door leading to the dark basement and explained that the straps used to punish mean kids were hanging on the wall down there. I didn't see any straps, but I figured they were there waiting to be used. Maybe she was joking, but I don't think any of us thought so. Five-year-olds are just not into that dry kind of humor. Who at that early age could forget such a frightening incident? So did this incredible tactic by Sister "What's Her Name" scare the daylights out of us? Of course it did. Did the scare tactic make us behave like perfect little children? Of course not! We were typical kids.

I remember that I launched spitballs on more than one occasion. The missiles were easily made out of those little cardboard letters used to teach us the alphabet. The inflexible nuns didn't care much about such activities. This misbehavior may be why I never learned the complete alphabet until much later—I mean really much later. I also have to admit that I loved to fight with other boys on the playground. The nuns didn't care too much about that either. Running in the halls seemed fairly innocuous, but it was another no-no. Being late for school was absolutely a mortal sin. Sometimes the tardiness was simply due to hanging out at the candy store across the street from the school gawking at the delicious-looking assortment of sugary items. When the tardiness occurred, one particular nun would grab you by the cheeks with a powerful hand and squeeze while she demanded to know why you were late. Of course you couldn't give an understandable answer to the question because of the death hold, all of which increased proportionally to the lack of an answer. It was a vicious catch-22 situation. I don't know why she couldn't understand the reason for our lack of cooperation to her interrogation.

Two years later, I escaped from Sister "Death Hold" and was enrolled in the third grade in the small community of Ivanhoe, Minnesota, located in the southwestern part of the state. I hated grade school here too, except for the indoor toilets. We didn't have indoor plumbing at home. We lived in the poorest area in the poorest town in the poorest county of Minnesota. It is interesting that I cannot remember the name of one of my grade school teachers—not one!

Most people usually remember their favorite grade school

teachers. I assume that my lack of memory in this regard is due to not having good grade school experiences. Grade school was where teachers gave out gold stars for various classroom accomplishments. I never received any gold stars. Some students got silver stars and some got red stars. I don't remember getting any stars. The nice kids with the new clothes, the perfect hygiene, indoor toilets in their homes, and sometimes a mushy relationship with the teacher got the stars. Shabby little kids from the edge of town by the railroad tracks without sewer facilities didn't get stars. This sounds like sour grapes; however, I should be a little honest and qualify things. These star-studded students did their assigned lessons, memorized everything that was supposed to be memorized, and followed teachers' instructions. Of course the teachers liked them.

Not getting stars was mostly my fault. Nonetheless, I wasn't impressed with such early grade school pedagogy. All I got was the fear of being held back in the same grade every year, the fear often perpetuated by the teacher. I think the teachers used this scare tactic to prompt me to do school work, but at the time I didn't know it. I was always scared to death at the end of each school year when the final dreaded report card came out. Schools did indeed hold kids back in those days. There was little or no attention given to the social aspects of not moving children on to the next grade with their classmates. Learn it or repeat it was the educational battle cry. There were kids in the sixth grade almost ready to shave.

One of the things that bothered me in grade school was all of that memorization. I certainly realize that memorization is part of the learning procedure, and therefore, it is a huge part of grade school. It is not a bad idea to know the alphabet. I knew parts of it fairly well. I was so embarrassed in college that I finally had to sit down and learn the entire alphabet. The number of days in each of the months proved to be another early hang up for me. I have finally solved this piece of intellect too. I don't know why I was so adverse to memorization. I could do it, but I just didn't do it. I wasn't a terribly bad student. I very much liked reading and arithmetic.

Let me point out a mockery of justice in the classroom that I recall very well. After taking a quiz, or even a significant exam, the students would be asked to exchange papers in order to correct each other's answers. That maneuver was bad enough, but then the teacher would record your grades by calling out your name and you would have to announce to the teacher and the entire class that you had only achieved 50 percent or 40 percent or even worse. I always wondered why they didn't put the information on the six o'clock radio news so everyone in the listening area would know how you performed. Of course, the little kiddies who did their homework and prepared well for class each day would enunciate their 80 and 90 percents loudly and with great delight. Even at this very early age in academics, I thought that something was wrong with this procedure—that we needed regulations, or maybe even a law. My scores were sometimes not too impressive because of my indifference to busy work and the fact that my parents were seldom around to push me to do it. However, some of the students lacked the ability to do well and couldn't have obtained a good score if you gave them the answers ahead of time. Why embarrass them? Even as a youngster from the town's outhouse district, I felt that this pedagogy was not right. Why couldn't teachers sense the embarrassment they were causing for some students. Individuals are not created equal in all academic regards.

So grade school didn't go well for me. At any rate, the phobia of being held back was finally over. I thought that maybe they didn't hold you back once you reached junior high school. Regardless, I now moved on to the next level in anticipation of being exposed to more teachers. I was hoping that teachers would be less prone to regimental procedures, more adaptable, and actually make learning fun.

One of our classes upon reaching junior high school, probably social studies, included a project whereby we all went to the Lincoln County Courthouse to look up some of our records. It was not much of a field trip because the courthouse was across the street from the school. I'm not sure whether this exercise was simply a normal social studies project or whether it was meant to make sure that our records were in order for a subsequent draft into the military. At any rate, the activity was fun, and it turned out to be a very bizarre day. I found out that I was going by the wrong name. My father's name was "Kowalewski," which I thought was my name, but my parents had baptized me "Kowles"—probably because many Polish people were shortening their name in those days. But I didn't know anything about the name change. My parents had never told me. I found out in the courthouse by way of a school project. My mother never explained this conundrum to me. Anyway, I attended school on Wednesday as "Kowalewski" and came back to school on Thursday morning as "Kowles." And my schoolmates could no longer call me "Kovie" because the nickname didn't fit anymore. The overnight change didn't concern me much at the time. Regardless of the name change, I was still the same person, for better or worse.

I thought junior high school would be more fun because we would actually have to do some thinking. To some extent, I was right, but a few of the teachers had trouble being competent. The World War II years probably took its toll on this occupation as it did on many others during this terrible time. Schools were getting by the best they could. Maintaining discipline seemed to be the biggest problem.

The school desks were on railings in sections of three or four seats. During one class period, students slowly moved a long section of these desks inch by inch in a coordinated action. The teacher didn't realize what was going on until this group of mischievous students almost disappeared from the classroom into the next room. On another occasion, several students dismantled a section of these desks during class by removing the screws and bolts. The desks were on the verge of collapsing by the time the creative students left for the next class. As a result, some of us innocent ones were threatened by the school disciplinarian that we should be sent to the state correction facility for juveniles in Red Wing, Minnesota. But it was the other guys. Really!

Junior high school chorus was made up of mostly girls, and the choral director desperately wanted to add some male voices to the group. Consequently, some of us were coerced into joining the chorus. I was never a joiner, but I thought what the heck, I would help out and give it a shot. After a few practices sessions, I was told to just move my lips, but don't actually make any sounds. I immediately quit. The insensitive music director would have to find some other male pawn to stand up there pretending to sing simply for the sake of having more pants on the stage.

Another problem I had in junior high school was the infamous quiz contest. The teacher would split the class into two groups, and the students would line up on opposite sides of the room like a tag match. Then the teacher would systematically bombard each student on the two sides with questions. If you got the answer wrong you had to sit down. The side with the last student(s) standing would win. Again it was embarrassing if you were early to sit down. I guess the strategy was that it would prompt students to study in order to avoid the embarrassment of being the first to sit down. Regardless, there will always be a first to sit down. I think the pedagogical master plan only made some students look foolish. At least they didn't make you stand in the corner of the room with a big sign and bold letters that read, "Dummy."

Not all of the teachers during this time period were troublesome. Some of them were quite good. One of the better teachers constantly gave me a hard time, always prodding me to do better. One time when she was relentlessly on my back, I rattled off some very unbecoming Polish at her that I had learned from my grandmother. I think the tirade was "God damn it, you're a big crazy dirty devil." She had an Irish name so I was sure that I would get away with it. However, she remembered much of what I said, had her Polish landlady translate it, and then assigned me to a considerable number of days after school.

This same teacher with the great memory taught geography, and in those days, you had to pass a state examination in geography before you were eligible for high school. She announced to the entire class that if anyone failed this exam, it would be me (damn her). I asked why and was told in front of the entire class that I was too independent to even follow directions. This branding ticked me off, so I studied hard, followed directions, and got the best score in the entire class. I felt like I showed her, but I bet she felt like she showed me. My entire class passed, and we were all headed for the big time in academia—high school.

Many years later while serving as the chairperson of the biology department at Saint Mary's University of Minnesota, I received a telephone call from a personnel director at a large department store (Dayton's) in Minneapolis. The woman asked me for a recommendation relative to a job applicant whom I had in several classes. After giving the former student a good recommendation, she thanked me and then asked whether I was the Kowles she had in the eighth grade. It was my geography teacher. Her final words of our conversation before hanging up were "I'm glad someone in that darn class made something of themselves." We must have driven her out of teaching.

Some teachers in our small high school in Ivanhoe, Minnesota, on the plains of southwestern Minnesota, were extraordinarily excellent. Mr. Harold Johnson made mathematics so clear and logical that one would be hard pressed not to like the subject. Mr. Arthur Clarin was my first biology teacher, and I give him credit as being the first person to impart an interest for the subject to me. He made me realize that the biological world was intriguing. Also on this small faculty was Mr. Donald DuBois. This guy was a tough, no nonsense English teacher. He was extremely intelligent, and he had an uncanny way of getting you to do a lot of academic work. We diagrammed sentences until we were doing them in our sleep. I was so fortunate to have such good teachers for the very essential subjects of mathematics, science, and English. They were also the catalysts in my thinking about ultimately becoming a teacher myself.

In undergraduate college at Winona State Teachers College

(now Winona State University), Joe Emanuel and M. R. Raymond furthered my interest in the sciences. Both were excellent lecturers demanding straight thinking and exactness from their students. In graduate school at the University of Minnesota, I enjoyed all of the professors in which I came into contact. They helped mold me into a genetics professor. I must confess, however, that I am probably quite biased in this regard because the subject matter was of such great interest to me. It was easy for me to like their presentations and to study for their examinations.

Chapter 3
Wanting to Teach

When I was a senior in high school, I read in the local newspaper that some of our more experienced teachers were making a salary of $3,600 per year. In such a small town, the *Ivanhoe Times* paper printed everything about everyone. I quickly calculated that these educational stalwarts were actually making $100 per week since the academic year was about thirty-six weeks long. To someone like myself living in the outhouse district, this seemed like big money. It was clean work, and you got to wear a white shirt and tie. It seemed like all you had to do was to sprinkle some chalk on a board a few times each day and, of course, keep the wild ones in the class under control. I already had some experience from the other side of the desk by being in a class that had its share of unruly students. I also noticed that teachers in my hometown were respected by the community. In addition, some of the teachers who taught me in high school definitely had an influence on me relative to pursuing a teaching career. Yes indeed, seeking a teaching career sounded like a great idea.

A realistic and sobering thought, however, kept creeping in. Becoming a teacher required a college degree. I realized that it was not a bad idea to begin saving money for college even during the early years of junior high school. But we were a poor family and saving money was difficult. Any money earned was used for shoes, a few clothes, and a little entertainment such as shooting pool (five cents a game), movies (ten cents a movie), and drinking pop (five cents a bottle). Even those expenses were not always easy to meet.

Collecting scrap iron was my first financial bonanza. People in my hometown had organized scrap iron drives for the World War II effort. Periodically a train would come through town with flatbed cars to pick up donated scrap iron. As a youngster, I was a loner in the scrap iron business, selling the metal that I collected by wandering around in the alleys and ditches with my little wheelbarrow. If I happened to come across some aluminum or copper, the find would generate sheer excitement—like discovering gold bullion. I probably only made a total of $20 or $30, but that amount was considerable relative to the times. Due to the war the speed limit was 40 or 45 miles per hour in order to save on rubber tires, and it was unpatriotic to drive any faster. In those trying days, food was rationed, especially meat and sugar along with other grocery items. Families were issued coupons each month for purchasing food items, and the coupons had to last until the next issue. The only plus in those difficult times was that junior high kids like myself could usually find work because so many people were serving in the military. The pay, however, was always atrociously low—even for wet-nosed youngsters. So none of my early financial ventures resulted in much of a monetary balance for college.

As a seventh grader, a farmer hired me to drive a big John Deere tractor that pulled a machine for cutting and bundling small grain (called a binder). The farmer sat on the binder watching the bundles of grain flying out from it. We cut grain from sunrise to sunset, and I was paid $2 per day. Of course, the farmer's wife fed me, and she was a heck of a good cook. Considering my appetite, the free food served as a significant bonus. One day we were cutting a large field of flax grain. Many farmers grew flax during the war years because of the high oil content in the grain. I asked the farmer how much money he got for the flax when he sold it. He said something like $6.80 or $7 per bushel. I nearly fell off the tractor. We cut and harvested a bushel of flax in three or four minutes. And he was paying me $2 per twelve- to fourteen-hour day. A couple of fields that we worked belonged to another farmer, and the terrain was dangerously steep with scattered gullies. I asked my farmer boss why we were risking our lives cutting the grain on those roller coaster fields belonging to someone else. The other farmer was afraid to cut the fields because they were so hilly. And I was risking my life for $2 per day. Needless to say, with wages like that no money was saved for college after this job either.

Being an experienced tractor driver landed me a similar job cutting grain with a different farmer the following summer for $4 per day. In a business sense, this wage was a 100 percent increase. That same fall, I drove a tractor for a road construction company contracted by the Minnesota State Highway Department to do a road repair project between Ivanhoe and Canby, Minnesota. I was an eighth grader working on a state highway project. Men were indeed scarce for these jobs during World War II.

A thrashing crew was still another source of income. In those days, farmers harvested their grain with a thrashing machine, not the newer invention called a combine. A huge leather belt ran from the machine to a large high horse-powered tractor that ran the noisy thrashing machine. But everything else was accomplished with real horses. I was given the job of driving the horse-drawn wagon that collected the grain from the machine. The horses given to me never responded to any commands, all of which resulted in several short distance runaways. The farmers who gathered to help each other with the harvest loved to give the young guy the most undisciplined team of horses. This bit of scheming was how they got their jollies. They thought it was a blast when you couldn't control the horses. I was a professional tractor driver, not a horseman. And I always felt that the horses never liked me. It was a personal thing between the horses and me. At any rate, I still had not saved any money for college.

For a couple of years early in high school, I worked in a small butcher shop/grocery store, part time during the school year and full time in the summer. The store was quite small and run by just the butcher owner and myself when he wasn't around. This experience indicated to me that I didn't deal well with the public. Most of the time the head guy did all the front business while expressing his humorous and likeable personality. I was relegated to the backroom boning out meat and making baloney, then cleaning up at the end of the day. But the butcher guy liked to take off occasionally leaving me in charge. Some of his older adult customers loved to pick on young people as if we were moronic. I always reciprocated their nastiness, sometimes telling them that they probably should shop at the other store down the street. Being a member of a relatively poor family and having a father struggling with the demons of alcohol and a mother who worked day and night trying to make ends meet were factors that led to a mood in which I didn't want to take flak from anyone, not even my elders. This personality flaw really bothered the boss man. Mr. butcher was between a rock and a hard place. He very much liked my work ethic, but he didn't want to lose customers because of the kid with the acid tongue behind the counter.

One time, the butcher boss really had a valid gripe. The priest from the Catholic parish in a neighboring small town wanted some choice T-bone steaks for an important dinner party that he was hosting. No steaks were available in the meat counter, and the butcher was out. But I knew that I could handle the situation. A quarter of beef was hanging in the walk-in cooler that looked to me like it had a great side of T-bone steaks. So I took charge and cut the good father a stack of T-bones. The steaks looked perfect and I was so proud; however, I didn't realize that the hunk of beef was very old bull meat to be used for making baloney. I found out by way of vehement complaints that the steaks were tougher than tree bark. That party must have been something to behold, probably punctuated with a lot of priests swearing at the kid in the butcher shop. If these priests had any influence with the Big One, I will surely go to hell. I really heard from the butcher who really heard from the priest who really heard from his guests. After all of this stress and gnashing of teeth, I still hadn't saved any money for college.

Eventually, I was able to gain employment on construction crews. These entry-level jobs are known as grunt work. You unload trucks, push a wheelbarrow, mix mortar, and dig—a lot of digging. The shovel becomes a major part of your life. Construction work was hard labor, but the hourly wage was decent. A good summer of work would normally allow one to have enough money to at least get started in college. I really wanted to go to college, and I really wanted to become a teacher. The profession sounded more interesting than driving tractor, making baloney, and wheeling cement. But early in the pivotal summer before college, misfortune struck. I broke my collarbone in two places and chipped my shoulder blade playing town team baseball. Consequently, I was out of work of any kind.

When fall arrived and it was time to head for college, the savings for college was miniscule. As the final time came to depart and make my mother proud, I told her that I needed to work during the next year and then think about going to college in the following year. In her patented firm way, she said: "Richard, you are going to college—get packed." Whenever she called me "Richard" I knew that she meant business. I responded that it was impossible to go to college because I didn't have any money. I didn't even have anything to pack. I asked my dear mother, who was almost as broke as myself, how this college aspiration was supposed to materialize. She pointed out in a matter of fact way that I would find a way. No one on her side of the family as far as you could do the genealogy had ever obtained a college degree. Mother was determined that I would be the first. Although I appreciated her faith in my being able to pull it off, I reiterated that I was in no position to go. Once more she said, "Go." So we compromised and I went.

With $34.30 I took off for college, actually arriving with $27.30 because the train ticket cost me $7. I distinctly remember these numbers because I thought that they might be of interest someday. Tuition in those days was $30 per quarter, so I didn't have to borrow much money from a friend for that first registration. Once I enrolled, I was awarded an academic scholarship that paid my tuition the rest of the way, which helped immensely. A four-year academic scholarship was not bad for someone who didn't quite know the whole alphabet. Soon after, I also received about $110 from the baseball team. I was hoping that this payment would not jeopardize my amateur standing for college athletics because I really liked to hang out in the gym and on various athletic fields. At any rate, I was on my way for the preparation to teach. Now all I needed was inexpensive board and room and a lot of part-time work during the school year, and a mother's prediction might be proven right.

During four years in college, I played three interscholastic sports, which included baseball. Continuing to play baseball the summer following graduation was easy to do because town baseball teams in the area were always happy to accept ex-college baseball players to their rosters. After one game during that summer, a Saint Louis Cardinal baseball scout approached me. He wanted me to go to an upcoming Cardinal baseball tryout camp. He said he watched me during a number of ball games and that I had a good chance of signing with the Cardinal organization. This possibility sounded exciting, but I had already signed a contract to teach in a high school on the Minnesota Iron Range that fall. More importantly, my wearing glasses because of myopia and astigmatism made it terribly difficult for me to hit good curve balls—even bad curve balls. Once the opposition became aware of this baseball Achilles heel, pitchers would quit throwing fastballs to me and instead give me a steady diet of the dreaded curve balls. This situation turned me into an ordinary batter. I didn't want to end up coaching third base in some mountain league at age fifty-something for pizza and beer money. Honest self-assessment and common sense prevailed, plus I really wanted a teaching career.

As a teacher, I knew that I could be involved in activities that I liked such as organizing, planning, being creative, reading, and studying. I had always felt that the activity of learning was actually fun, if it wasn't simply busy stuff. And what an interesting, difficult, joyful, eventful, challenging career teaching turned out to be.

Chapter 4

Working My Way through College

Choosing a college was an interesting adventure. Because of some notable success in high school athletics, several colleges actively recruited me to attend their institution. Some of my acquaintances and relatives advised me to go to LaCrosse State College (now University of Wisconsin—LaCrosse) because the college had a thriving sports program at the time. However, this college never recruited me. Augsburg College in Minneapolis recruited me by mail for their field and track program. The University of Minnesota dined me in the Twin Cities and introduced me to some of their All-Americans and even their 1941 Heisman Trophy recipient, Bruce Smith, to recruit me to try out for its football team. Saint Thomas College (now University of Saint Thomas) offered me free tuition (an academic scholarship) for the freshman year if I would play football. I asked about free tuition for subsequent years if I happened to blow out a knee and couldn't play football anymore. The recruiter wasn't sure what would happen under such circumstances. I wasn't able to pay tuition at a state college, let alone a private college. Consequently, this recruitment interaction ended abruptly. So I enrolled at Winona State Teachers College (now Winona State University) in Winona, Minnesota, because I was offered an academic scholarship with no athletic strings attached. I just needed to keep up my grades. I could participate in interscholastic athletics simply if I wanted to do so. And I really wanted to do so.

I knew that going to college would still be a monumental financial challenge for me. At age seven, because of domestic problems, my parents shipped me from our rented apartment in Winona, Minnesota, to my widowed grandmother in Ivanhoe, a little community of 606 residents located across the state in southwestern Minnesota. Once again this town was deemed by some sources to be one of the poorest towns in one of the poorest counties in the state of Minnesota. And I also thought that Grandmother's house was on one of the poorest streets in the town. So for a few years before my parents temporarily reconciled and joined me in Ivanhoe, my grandmother raised me. In my mind, Grandmother was a saint, a staunch Catholic woman of Polish heritage. She was born in the United States about four years after her parents arrived at Ellis Island from Poland. She became a widow at a relatively early age, losing her husband, one son, and her father within a span of about two years. In spite of this rash of setbacks, she carried on without public assistance.

Grandmother had a little income from leasing several small parcels of farmland that she had inherited to farmers. Beyond that, survival meant a large garden, some fruit trees, canning just about everything, and a small flock of chickens for eggs, drumsticks, and soup. Her house had a furnace, but most of the heat came from a kitchen stove fueled by wood that I chopped all summer long and remnant coal that dropped from the steam engine locomotives alongside the railroad tracks not far from the house. I would scrape the coal up into a pail and haul it back to the house. When someone would tell me that I might get sticks and coal for Christmas, which I probably deserved, I was elated. The chickens were mostly fed with corn and wheat that I scraped up from the area surrounding the large grain elevators also down by the railroad tracks. I was a premier scavenger. I never knew whether these survival activities were legal or not.

Eventually, my parents, younger brother, and I became a family again (sort of) in little Ivanhoe. My mother had completed training for beautician work, and she opened a little shop in town. My father, always fighting the demons of alcohol, worked only sporadically as a day laborer obtaining some miscellaneous jobs. It was excruciatingly obvious that almost the entire financial burden of going to college would rest upon me and only me.

After arriving in Winona to attend college in the fall of 1950, I still had to find a place to eat and sleep. Mary M. was a sweet elderly lady who ran a boarding house about five blocks from the college campus. Mary's mother, also a sweet even more elderly lady, helped Mary prepare lunch and dinner every day for about twelve men, mostly college students. Lunch and dinner was ninety cents per day. What a break! However, it was four academic years of mostly Spam at lunchtime and mostly pork steak at dinnertime. Even at this low cost, the payment for this subsistence was often far in arrears. But some of us were willing to endure just about anything to obtain a college education.

A large three-story house owned by the college a few blocks from the campus turned out to be a great place to rent a room. About twenty college students roomed at the place. It was a stately house with large living and dining rooms where the students could chat, read papers, and play cribbage. I recall that it cost about $13 per month.

After checking in the first day, my assigned roommate sprawled out on his bunk and stared at the ceiling of the room. He was from some place in northern Minnesota and was already so tremendously homesick. This affliction occurred before the end of the first day. Personally, I felt excited along with a touch of freedom and went to a beer party the very first night in town. Day two arrived and my roommate was long gone. His parents, bless their souls, picked him up and took him home.

No tuition worries, my room was only $13 per month, and board was only 90 cents per day. But still those few dollars were hard to come by. I, like many others, needed to find part-time work, a lot of part-time work. Then, of course, there were those students who would simply contact their parents with a straightforward message: send more money. Jeez how we disliked those people, but it would have been great to be one of them.

One rather serious problem arose while rooming at the Winona State College house. As active young men and usually broke, we were always hungry. The large house shared by fifteen or twenty college students was empty for the Thanksgiving holiday break except for two of us. I had basketball practice, and the other guy had a part-time job at one of the local business establishments so neither of us could go home.

A package arrived for one of the student tenants who, of course, had already gone home for Thanksgiving. The box from his parents surely looked like food, and the word "perishable" was boldly printed on it. We were hungry, showing some pity for ourselves because it was Thanksgiving, and the box was labeled as perishable. Upon breaking postal regulations, we found the contents to indeed be food: bananas, cookies, candy, and so forth. After devouring this guy's food, we began to realize that we were going to be in big trouble. Before the victim of this devious act returned, we purchased some bananas, cookies, candy, and so forth to replace the foodstuffs in a poorly wrapped package.

Being very angry about the prank, this student took the issue to the college dean and even threatened to go to the U.S. Postal Service. Getting dismissed from the college or even going off to jail entered our moronic minds, all because of some bananas, cookies, candy, and so forth. The end result was a hearing with a college council composed of some faculty and a few students that was established for minor disciplinary problems. We bribed several of the students on the council with beer, and the whole matter was dropped after some appropriate apologies. And I survived the first quarter of my freshman year.

Mary M.'s meals were served in her dining room. The student boarders would gather in the living room until Mary would call us to chow down. Twelve very hungry men would sit around a large oval table and eat in a family-style manner, passing around the various trays of bread, potatoes, celery, and, of course, Spam. Mary usually replenished platters of potatoes and bread when empty. Meat was obviously the most expensive item and when this platter was clear, it remained clear.

At one particular lunch, the meat platter began its round just to my right, and everyone showed great delight in taking a little more meat than his share. When the platter finally reached me at the end of its journey around the table, Mary would not have had to wash it. Everyone got a good laugh as I stuffed my face with boiled potatoes and white bread. Mary's reaction was that college boys have to be college boys.

At dinner that evening, I made a point to arrive at Mary's place first and sit close to the dining room entry. When Mary called us to the table, I was the first one into the dining room and strategically located myself where the platter of pork steak was on the table. Yes indeed I scraped a lot of the meat from the platter onto my plate and passed the sparsely scattered meat platter onward. And the pork orgy began. I ate most of it, probably a good portion of a loin from a large hog and waddled away in gluttonous triumph. The message was supposed to be that my fellow diners shouldn't mess with me when it came to food. But several of the boarders never forgave me. And Mary just responded once again with that college-boys-need-to-be-college-boys look on her face.

Necessary labor while in college began with filleting walleyes in a fish market. Large crates of whole fish packed in crushed ice would arrive by truck. Cats and dogs would follow me down the street after a few hours in that workplace. I only lasted ten days before the employer realized his business would thrive without my fleshing out his fish.

The college also gave me part-time jobs. I believe this gesture of support was because I liked to chase a football like dogs chase sticks and Frisbees. In the locker room, I got to fold sweat socks returned from the laundry (thankfully returned from the laundry). That position wasn't very high tech, and it paid thirty-five cents per hour. Cleaning blackboards in the classrooms of the main building every night was ho-hum, but I was elated that they trusted me with a master key. It made me feel really important. Cleaning the terrazzo with a brush and soapy water along the base of the hallways was the pits. This job was simply invented to keep you busy. I never found the darn terrazzo dirty, but I had to scrub it anyway. After all if you are going to rake in thirty-five or forty cents per hour, you have to earn the generous wage. Shoveling sidewalks in the winter for rich people in the neighborhood was okay, but these elderly, well-off people were extremely picky. They wanted every little piece of ice removed no matter how tenaciously it was adhering to the cement sidewalk.

Removing the flesh from mink pelts on a mink farm south of the city was a highly stressful job. The pelts were turned inside out and frozen. We had to scrape the flesh off of them while frozen without making any tears in the very expensive fur. If you didn't go fast enough, you got yelled at. If you went fast and tore the fur, you got yelled at. The job only lasted a few days because it was seasonal, and the big mink harvest always occurred during the college's Thanksgiving break. Scraping stinking mink pelts and eating peanut butter sandwiches for lunch on Thanksgiving Day didn't leave me with much to be thankful about. And once again the dogs and cats would follow me down the street upon returning to town each evening.

Scrubbing floors and restocking the coolers with beer in a local bar at 5:00 a.m. every morning was not a lot of fun either. I had to free the floors from the stale beer that was slopped all over the place during the previous night, probably by some of my own beer-drinking friends. Upon completion of this less than aromatic task, I smelled like beer and the dogs and cats once again followed me down the street as I walked back to my residence. One's commitment to obtain a college degree can really be tested.

Some of the part-time jobs were not too bad. Working for the post office during the Christmas season rush was actually fun. I got to ride in one of those little postal vehicles all over the city delivering packages, everywhere from tar paper shacks in the woods at the edge of town to the multimillionaire's mansion in the center of the city. Jeez how I wanted to get a good look at the interior of that millionaire's house, but the butler quickly took the package from me at the door and slammed the door in my face. I thought that butlers were only in the movies.

Being a gunner at the local dog club was an easy job. Another worker would throw a dead pigeon into the air, and I would simultaneously shoot a shotgun into the air. Then I would have to stand absolutely motionless while the dog's owner/trainer at some distance away from me would direct his prize dog with a whistle to the downed pigeon. Some of those dogs were smarter than a few of the people in my sphere of acquaintances.

Painting window frames in a five-story building in the downtown area of Winona evolved into an interesting experience. My college student colleague and I were not union members. We were two college kids who just wanted to make a few bucks. This situation posed a problem for the painters' union and, of course, we got picketed. There they were, the picketers prancing back and forth with their signs underneath where I was painting. I just couldn't resist. So I would *accidentally* spill a little paint in their direction from time to time. The picketers, therefore, moved to the other side of the street that was in front of an empty lot. After their relocation, it appeared that they were picketing against the large weeds in the empty lot. We finished the job without any further incidences and got some of our bills paid.

Another part-time job (almost full time) while attending a full load of classes and playing varsity football consisted of a five-hour shift (8:00 p.m. to 1:00 a.m.) in a factory Monday through Friday. This job was the making of huge oil filters about three feet long to be used in diesel locomotives. The task consisted of packing large sack-like tubes with some kind of fibrous material. I was not very good at making those oil filters. I was slow, and when I finally completed them, many of the filters were monstrosities. A diesel locomotive wouldn't make it out of town with such an oil filter. It kind of looked like a large penis that needed a whole lot of Viagra. Many of my filters were probably rejects. Most of the women on the manufacturing line made the filters quickly, and they were perfectly constructed. Still I received ninety cents per hour because I was a male, and the females on the line received seventy-five cents per hour simply because they were females.

According to a lot of employers, women were in the workforce to make some extra egg money. I felt sorry for the women having to put up with such an inequity; it was sociological injustice based on what toilet we used. I even questioned the foreman concerning this disparity, but to no avail. He didn't have anything to do with the financial side of the company, and I was never able to determine the identity of the big guy. The women appreciated my well-meaning feelings about the situation. But alas, I took the ninety cents per hour wage because I had to pay for the Spam. I only lasted two or three months on that job. Being a full-time student with a need to protect an academic scholarship, playing varsity football, and working a five-hour shift every night Monday through Friday was a rather inhumane schedule. Besides when in college, one must find some time to imbibe a little amber-colored liquid with your classmates. It is part of college culture.

Summer time was a welcomed time when one could find a good-paying job for three months and make some significant, well-needed money. I was hired by a construction company involved in building curbs and gutters in a town near my hometown. It was hard work and at times very monotonous. One time during some down time I sat in the bucket of one of those large front-end loading machines while the operator raised it to the top of a tall thick hedge so that I could view a young woman in her backyard getting a sun tan on all parts of her body. Everyone has occasional moments of juvenility.

A couple of summers were spent working for a silo building company with its home office also located in a neighboring town. I would drive my 1932 Chevy seventeen miles one way on an old gravel road to get to the workplace. I was a very proud owner of that automobile, already twenty years old in 1952. The vehicle had pull down shades on the windows, wooden spokes on the wheels, and a horn that was a sheer delight to blow. Building silos was also hard labor, but I didn't mind because I wanted to get into great physical shape for the fall football season. Most of the silos were built in the farmlands and cattle country of South Dakota. The alkaline-tasting drinking water was the worst part of the job. I was the guy on the round scaffold within and at the top of the silo, ascending with the scaffolding periodically as the silo increased in height. I would have to pull each concrete stave up with a motorized boom, grab the thirty-five-pound whirling mass of concrete, and work it into place on the edge of the silo.

Our crew would work from sunrise to sunset Monday through Saturday amounting to nearly eighty hours per week. Such a schedule meant forty hours at $0.95 per hour and another forty hours at time and a half ($1.425 per hour). The long hours didn't interfere with entertainment because out in the farmlands of South Dakota there wasn't any entertainment. The farmer (actually his wife) would always feed us wherever we worked, and this part of the job was heaven on earth for a group of hard-working young men. Sometimes there would be chicken, steak, and a pork roast on the table, all at one meal. These farm people definitely knew how to feed a working crew.

One hazard on the job, other than the possibility of falling to your death, was the guy on the ground hooking the staves on the cable for me to pull up. He would occasionally smear the concrete stave with pig poop; it was always in great supply around the construc-tion of silos. It was not possible to detect the awful stuff on the stave before grabbing it as it ascended in a twirling motion. I would save the porky waste until I had enough to form a small bomb about the size of a baseball. When the jokester on the ground wasn't looking, it was bombs away. I was surprised at the accuracy from forty feet or more above ground level.

One summer I wanted to work on the barges traveling up and down the Mississippi River. It seemed like an exciting job, at least in my naïve way of thinking. However, a different job opportunity opened up first in the Twin Cities, and I grabbed it, not taking a chance on being completely left out of summer work.

Working on the assembly line in the Ford plant in Saint Paul was one heck of an experience. The plant was a closed shop, meaning that everyone had to belong to the union. I was okay with joining because I was never antiunion. Besides, the wages were the best that I had ever received (something like $2.50 per hour). But after doing exactly the same task every minute of eight-hour days, five days a week for three months, I darn well knew that I had to finish college. When the efficiency expert came around with his clipboard and stopwatch, I showed him how fast I could work. I was really efficient and also really stupid. The result of this idiocy was another task assigned to me as those automobile frames came streaming by on the assembly line. The assembly line was like eternity. It never stopped. I thought that if you would lead a naughty life on earth, you would go to hell and work on the Ford assembly line in Saint Paul for all eternity.

Big Ed and I bolted down the rear end transmissions onto the frames as they approached us. He did one side and I did the other side. Big Ed liked the job. He had been doing this same task for six years, and he was making good money by his standards. He belonged to the union, of course, and therefore, he felt that he could screw around as much as he wanted to without company repercussions. Once in a while, he would prove his immunity from being fired due to union membership by placing the wrong rear end transmission onto the frame—on purpose. Eleven transmissions existed that were clearly tagged to match the clearly tagged frame. One didn't have to be the sharpest knife in the drawer to make the match, but Big Ed would occasionally do a wrong match for the fun of it.

Farther down the line, an inspector would eventually detect the mismatch after much of the vehicle was already assembled. Extra workers would miraculously rush out of the woodwork and descend upon the automobile like a bunch of flies heading for horse poop. The auto would be torn down and correctly reassembled as the line continued to move. The line never stops. Once everything was rectified, the foreman, Swaney, would march over to Big Ed with his jaw jutting out about six inches to read him the riot act. Swaney always knew that it was Big Ed and not the befuddled college kid. Big Ed would simply respond that he made a mistake. After Swaney would leave still huffing and puffing, Big Ed would let go with a good laugh to cap off his big prank. Big Ed belonged to the union, and the company couldn't do anything about the problematic episode. It was simply a *mistake.*

The company and the union employees hated each other. Neither entity would give an inch to the other beyond what was etched in stone in the contract between them. I experienced this animosity in both directions. My job required using some heavy plates located about twenty or thirty feet away from the assembly line. I could only carry a few at a time, and then I would have to work frantically to catch up again on the moving frames. After catching up, I would have to run over to the bin and get some more of those heavy plates. This dilemma went on all day. So on this one particular morning at about 7:50 a.m. while waiting for the line to start at 8:00 a.m., I suddenly got the bright idea to pile a bunch of the plates by the line before it started up. I thought that I might get enough piled up to last me until almost lunchtime. Before 8:00 a.m. even arrived, I had union officials wearing long trench coats tapping me on the shoulder telling me not to do that. The reasoning explained to me was that I was giving the company more than eight hours, that is, a whole extra ten minutes. My sociological instincts prompted me to explain how I was just making my day brighter. They reiterated in no uncertain terms that I should not do that. At this point, I realized that I had carried things far enough and agreed with the nice gentlemen that I ought not do that.

The company was just as hard-nosed as the union. Employees were allowed a ten-minute break in the morning and another ten-minute break in the afternoon. These were the rules evidently agreed upon between the company and the union. However, the relief guy would start relieving immediately at 8:00 a.m. and work his way through part of the line in sequence, except that he would start each shift at a different place in the line. Therefore, you could get your break from 8:00 to 8:10 when you haven't even done any work yet, and not another until the short lunchtime period.

This situation happened to me one day, and at about 11:00 a.m. I really had to go number two. Swaney said: "Tough luck, you had your break already." So I vividly described to Swaney the pile of human waste that I was going to leave right next to the assembly line, kind of like from one rear end to another rear end. Swaney quickly rushed in a relief man to my aid. Considering everything, however, Swaney was a good guy, and we eventually got along very well.

On my last day, he took me to the office to get my last updated check cut, patted me on the back, shook my hand, and wished me good luck with my college career and teaching ambitions. I practically did handsprings and cartwheels all the way to my beat up 1947 Ford coup in the parking lot and headed back to Winona for another year of college. I fully realized that college was a wonderful place to hang out. Even the Spam sounded good again. I told many of my acquaintances that the Ford plant would fold without me. This prediction was boldly made was in 1953. The Ford plant in Saint Paul was completely closed down in 2012.

Other small incomes (very small) during the academic year came from refereeing high school basketball games, building sandbag dikes for the city of Winona during springtime flooding, and so forth. And in real desperate times, a local bank would loan me a few hundred dollars without asking for any collateral. Even some of my student colleagues would loan me small amounts of money. I diligently kept a record of those debts from friends, regardless of how small some of them were, and eventually paid every dollar back. Still, I left college with a total debt of a little more than two thousand dollars, which seemed immense at the time.

Chapter 5

The Preparation to Teach

College academics were new and interesting experiences and in some respects beyond my expectations. The mathematics professor walked into the lecture room on day one of the first quarter and collected our registration cards indicating our names and proof that we belonged in his trigonometry class. He didn't know any of us because we were mostly freshmen. He looked at the cards one by one (about twenty or twenty-five), called out our names, and associated our name on the card with our face. Then he set the cards aside and called us by our correct name, backward from how the cards were handed to him. You can imagine how that stunt impressed a wet-nosed kid from a small farm community who was mostly anxious to attend football practice. Later, I learned that this mathematics professor was in U.S. Army intelligence during World War II. It is no wonder that we won the war.

In those days, grade inflation did not exist. Many professors graded on strict curves, that is, a small percentage of the students would get "A" grades, a few more received "B" grades, most got "C" grades, the number of "D" grades were close to the number of "B" grades, and "F" grades were not at all unusual. Also, there was very little, if any, accountability. Professors were czars on the campus. They could do whatever they wanted to do. Student evaluations did not exist. The history professor babbled all term about nonsensical irrelevant things, like how thumbs help us hold soup spoons, until the final few days of the term. He then attempted to cover all of western civilization in two periods. And you were expected to know it. The English professor was anti-athletics. He didn't believe that any athlete could do well in his grammar course. After attaining mostly "A" grades the entire term, he told me that I would get a "B" or a "C" grade because I was in athletics. I was happy to get the "B" grade from the gentleman guilty of severe discrimination. Another history teacher also showed a distinct paranoid behavior. We called the head football coach "blood and guts" because it fit his demeanor well, but he was a really nice guy. He just had a little trouble making complete sentences. One of the physical education instructors couldn't look at me in class. He always spoke to the ceiling rather than directly to the students. And then there was the Fulbright scholar—not sure how that happened.

The professor of psychology was a prison psychologist earlier in his career. His prison stories were interesting entertainment, some of which were quite coarse. In music appreciation, the professor would play phonograph records of classical music, and he would often ask me what went through my mind as I listened to the music. My answer was always the same regardless of the piece being played: a herd of wild horses stampeding over the prairie. He probably continually picked on me in an effort to get some thought from me other than wild horses stampeding over the prairie. In art appreciation, I received one of the better grades for the abstract watercolor painting of a grouping made up of an apple, an orange, a candle, and so forth. I was completely clueless about what abstract meant, and I tried to paint the grouping exactly as it appeared. Later the art instructor said mine was really abstract, and she gave me a good grade.

I broke my leg in a pick-up basketball game, and the college nurse gave me two aspirins, told me to walk home, and come back to see her the next day. Instead I went to the emergency room at the local clinic and had a cast placed on my leg because it was determined that the fibula was cracked in two places. Of course, she didn't know the seriousness of the accident, but some students were very upset about this incident—concerned about incompetence. Nonetheless, I liked most of these interesting and colorful people.

The physiologist talked very slowly and distinctly in the laboratory in order to be precise with his instructions. He previously had been an army major or colonel, and things had to be done exactly the right way, which was his way. We all sat in the laboratory holding a live frog given to us for the experiment of the day. I think we were going to measure muscle contraction. The professor slowly pointed out that "first . . . [pause] . . . we need . . . [pause] . . . to kill . . . [pause] . . . the frog." By the time he finished the sentence with his slowly given instruction, the student next to me, a linebacker on the football team, had already killed the frog. One good whack on the edge of the lab table did it. This killing procedure was not exactly what the professor had in mind. You have to pith frogs by running a sharp needle-like probe into their brain (that kills them) and then the needle is sent down the spinal cord (that prevents reflex actions). These directions, however, came much too late. You cannot hold back uncontrollable laughter when such an event occurs.

Philosophy class was a blast too. I never really understood much about philosophy. So I would complete assigned papers by writing the craziest, most absurd, ridiculous thoughts that I could conjure up. The professor liked the stuff, and I got good grades in the course. The teacher who taught speech courses was tough. The class I attended was small, and consequently we had to give a short speech almost every class period. I subjected my fellow classmates to many of my unusual, and sometimes weird, experiences. Even this tough teacher with high standards seemed to enjoy my stories; however, she was never at a loss to show me in no uncertain terms how I could improve my speaking ability.

Joe Emanuel was the biology teacher who played a major role in piquing my interest in biology. I began as a double major in physical education and mathematics. Physical education seemed like a perfect fit because of my interest in sports and my participation in varsity athletics. And math was always a favorite subject of mine. Mathematics seemed so logical, and it was very objective rather than a lot of subjective nonsense. But after taking a number of biology courses, I decided this was an area of science that I wanted to pursue. It was about this time when biology was evolving from mostly leaf collections and bird watching to DNA, its role in genetics, its chemical structure, and its revolution of all biology. The genetic aspects of the discipline were becoming highly exciting, and it included some of the other academic areas that I liked such as statistics, mathematics, and chemistry.

I never got very enthused about the education courses that were required in my curriculum. I didn't think that I was learning much about how to handle a class of high school students. Without having any teaching experience yet, I still had strong feelings that one would learn how to teach on the job. Consequently, I was probably bordering on being rebellious with regard to taking these courses. In a course called *Observation*, I was supposed to go to other schools in the city and observe various classes. Instead I often went golfing. In a course called *Visual Arts*, I was supposed to learn how to make posters and other trivial displays. Instead I often skipped class and went golfing. The visual arts assignments that I turned in at the end of the course were absolutely atrocious. A first grader would have been embarrassed with such a performance. Hence, I received "D" grades in both of these courses. These were the only "D" grades I ever got. Educational philosophy was a bore too, but I was endowed with enough asinine baloney to get by. I blame my distaste for these educational courses mostly on the biased attitude I had. When I now consider the mistakes that I made early in my teaching career, maybe more attention to educational aspects and less to golfing would have been a good thing.

Beyond going to classes and engaging in the social life connected with college, there were also sports. Spending an enormous amount of time on various athletic fields and gymnasiums was another significant part of my college life. I can't say enough about the rewards of college athletics. My scholarship was an academic one, and therefore, a certain level of good grades had to be maintained regardless of playing three varsity sports a year. Athletics certainly added to a very busy college life, but they also kept me interested in something other than class work. A college athlete can make a lot of friends and occasionally some enemies. People from all segments of the community were friendly, and almost everyone greeted me warmly. A few sports enthusiasts would even invite me to dinner in their homes. Still another factor in wanting to play sports is that some of us just relished the chance to crash into other people. During those bleak periods when I was penniless and seriously thinking of dropping out of school, it was often the next football or basketball game that kept me hanging in there, not the next social studies lecture.

College athletics allowed this small-town bumpkin to see parts of the country besides southern Minnesota and Sioux Falls, South Dakota. Even Iowa, North Dakota, Wisconsin, and Illinois were interesting places to this country guy. During my freshman year, I began stealing towels from the hotels where the team stayed if the hotel's name was on it. I ended a college career with quite a collection of towels. I knew this thievery was juvenile. The Wartburg Hotel in Iowa was not one of my favorite lodging places. The hallways were warped into the shape of a roller coaster, and the fire escape was a rolled up rope tied to the radiator by the window.

After a game in Dubuque, Iowa, the coach emphatically laid down the law; no one was to go over to East Dubuque, Illinois. As soon as we showered and dressed, we crossed the river and went over to East Dubuque. While there, I counted close to thirty bars on one particular street. A person could go from one bar to another without even going outside. At one bar where we decided to have a beer, a guy who looked like someone from *Guys and Dolls* wearing the dark suit with a nice gangster-type hat and bright tie reached across the bar to grab some bar peanuts. His handgun inside his suit coat became clearly visible. It also became apparent that we should keep our mouths shut and quickly get our butts back to the hotel on the other side of the river.

Football is hard on the body. One could really get beat up every Saturday night. On Sunday morning, it was very difficult to get out of bed. The situation often became a good excuse not to go to church. God would certainly understand, right? Around noon, I could ease out of the bunk and begin to slowly move around. Switching from football to basketball, supposedly a noncontact sport, was not easy. I turned out to be excellent at fouling. In fact, I fouled out of most games. The problem was my opponent's fault. They would try to shoot the ball. I couldn't stand to see my opponent shoot the ball. My exuberance sometimes brought on a chorus of boos.

Committing fouls, however, was not the only time that I got booed. Some supposedly well-meaning opponents would make the sign of the cross before they shot their free throws. I really hated that practice. What were they thinking? Were they asking God to help them defeat my teammates and me? Consequently, on several occasions I stepped into the lane and provided my own version of the sign of the cross followed by an arm signal to cancel the shooter's message. The crowd would usually boo, even at home games. The referee would tell me to quit. He said that I was inciting the crowd. Why couldn't I ask for a little help from God? God certainly knew that we needed as much help as anyone. The outcome that I still vividly remember about these incidents is that the free thrower invariably made the free throw after we exchanged signs of the cross. What did this say about my relationship with the Big One?

Varsity baseball was still another avenue for the release of energy and interesting episodes, some with a definite sociological twist. Our team would embark each spring on a southern trip. My first awakening experience in the South was going from the hotel where we stayed to a downtown location on a city transit bus. I always sat in the back of the bus. It was a habit. So when everyone was staring at me, I suspected that my zipper was open, the rear end of my pants had ripped open, or I was naïve with regard to their rules and regulations. Eventually I realized it was the latter situation. As snowballs, my two teammates and I were sitting in the back of the bus, which apparently was a no-no. After this revelation of sociology, we decided the hell with it and refused to move.

One sunny afternoon while playing an all-white college (because blacks were not allowed), I was playing first base, and the student body of the opposition was behind me sitting on a naturally sculptured hill giving me a hard time. Calling me a *damn Yankee* was actually the best of the derogatory blurts sent my way. Between innings, first basemen usually warm up the other infielders by throwing ground balls to each of them. Our player at third base had a rocket for an arm. So I threw a ground ball to him, and in his usual manner, he fired a laser to me. I missed the ball on purpose, and it went into the aggregation of fans sitting on the hillside. That incident prompted a real furor among the natives and increased the boisterous name-calling. Our coach gave me an earful too: "What the heck are you doing? We just want to win this game and get out of town."

If one is going to become a teacher, you have to engage in practice teaching. And you were expected to dress accordingly during this important preparation. I owned one sport coat that color-wise went fairly well with one pair of pants. A close friend, also practice teaching at the time, had a similar wardrobe combination but with different colors. For diversity, we would occasionally exchange sport coats. Our pants didn't fit each other, so our second outfit in both cases was a terrible color combination. In the classroom, I had no idea what I was doing. Still it appeared that the students liked me.

In spite of my self-evaluation indicating a moderate teaching ineptitude and room for plenty of improvement, I received a "B" grade. I think the kindness was partly due to the fact that I sold my beautiful Ithaca 12-gauge shotgun to the supervising teacher for a song because I needed the money.

Many interesting life experiences also occurred outside of the classroom during the college years. Beer drinking seemed to be a common theme. Almost everyone drank too much beer while in college. However, except for ethanol, I don't recall any other drugs being used by anyone in my sphere of acquaintances. I don't even recall anyone drinking hard liquor. Guzzling cheap beer was synonymous with college. A large bottle of beer, called a picnic bottle, was only sixty-five cents and would last an entire afternoon while sitting on the beach. The beer bottle looked like it contained about a half-gallon, and it was called "Bubs." This beer was the best laxative ever placed on the market. Upon returning to my boarding room house one very late winter evening, I found one of the college guys lying in the snow-covered bushes. He must have imbibed some potent hard liquor, but I never knew. It was a very cold night (about 15 degrees below zero), and he most certainly would have died had I not showed up. About thirty years later, I ran into him in a grocery store. He related to me how he became a born-again person. Then he started to preach to me, which turned me off. Heck, I was the sober one who saved his life.

And then there was another college acquaintance who had one heck of a talent, especially after a good night of beer drinking. He could urinate over a two-lane state highway without a drop touching the road. Once several of us were at a dance hall. The dance hall was crowded, and the adjacent parking lot to the dance hall was full of parked cars. Upon coming out of the hall to get some fresh air, someone asked Super Bladder whether he could hit the first row of cars in the lot. The considerable distance was deemed to be a challenge even for the peeing champion, but he did it—all over the windshield of one of the cars. Immediately, two heads of the opposite sex popped up in the car and the windshield wipers went on.

Through all of the shoestring finances, part-time jobs, turmoil, sweat, and tears, graduation eventually came about. Commencement was kind of a sad day. I loved college, and I loved Winona, and I had so many friends who I didn't want to leave. However, the college indicated that I had a degree, and that I must get out. Relatives of the graduates showed up in droves for the big commencement day. I didn't have one relative attend—not even relatives who lived in the same city. I walked across the stage, picked up my diploma, went back to my rented room, and took a nap. My thoughts were that a new series of episodes in schools would be starting soon, and that more fun would certainly come about.

A view of Winona, Minnesota, taken from a hilltop. The interstate bridge can be seen spanning the Mississippi River to the Wisconsin side. Winona is largely surrounded by water on three sides.
(Courtesy of Saint Mary's University of Minnesota)

The buildings making up Winona State University are shown in the center of the photograph. The athletic fields are in the foreground.

(Courtesy of Chops Hancock)

Chapter 6
The Anxiety of Job Hunting

The superintendent of the small school district located west of Rochester, Minnesota, was a serious guy, upper middle-aged with wire-rimmed glasses placed low on his prominent nose. He seemed keenly interested in my becoming an employee in his school district. We talked for a while, and eventually I had to ask him about some of the specifics concerning my workload. He rattled off a litany of responsibilities, some of which sounded more like chores making me a bit worried and almost dizzy. You will teach this. You will teach that. You will be in charge of this. You will take care of that. You will be involved in this. You will have hall duty, and so forth. At this point, I calmly asked whether I should be counted on to help wash dishes after the hot lunch program each day. There was a rather long moment of silence, and then he blurted out, "You don't want this job, do you?" I respectfully responded that he was very perceptive. An abrupt end of my first interview took place, and I was still jobless.

It is an interesting situation when at the time of graduation from college your thinking is that you are kind of special, and that everyone with a job opening is going to really compete for your services. The rude awakening, however, is that you are the one who is going to have to compete. Actually there didn't seem to be a surplus of teaching employment opportunities in 1954. And not wanting to leave Minnesota, or at the very least the Midwest region, didn't help my job hunting. The job search for that first teaching position generated a great deal of anxiety, and as time moved on, the anxiety began to transform into genuine stress.

I talked to someone about a teaching position in Fulda, Minnesota, located in the southwestern part of Minnesota. The discussion was mostly centered around taking care of their swimming pool, giving swimming lessons, and playing baseball for their summer town team. I don't recall much information given to me about the actual teaching job. It appeared like they were more interested in obtaining someone to play first base during the summer months. Besides that, when it comes to swimming, I estimate myself as a 5 on a scale of 10. This meant that I could save my own life if I was fairly close to shore and the current wasn't too strong.

On one occasion while in college, a friend and I were canoeing on the Mississippi River on a beautiful sunny afternoon—and of course sipping on beer. We accidentally rolled the canoe and had to swim to shore. It was not a problem for my friend because he was an excellent swimmer, but I thrashed pretty hard to make it. In fact, the other guy even swam back and retrieved the canoe, albeit the twelve-pack of beer was lost. Ironically, many years later this good swimmer drowned in the same Mississippi River while duck hunting.

I then received an invitation to interview for a teaching position in Keewatin, Minnesota, on the Iron Range. The Iron Range was a booming industry at that time. Good ore was being mined, people were making money, and the school districts had more than adequate budgets. With a freshly cut butch haircut, the only suit I owned, and a tie that didn't match anything, I headed north hoping that the superintendent and I would like each other. The first thing I found out is that Minnesota is a very long state, and I was still a hundred miles or more from the Canadian border. I had never been on the Iron Range before, and the topography looked mountainous. However, the big hills were composed of the material scraped off the source of the good iron ore. Big Euclid trucks dumped the rock and taconite materials at these locations; hence they were called dumps.

This interview went much better than my first ill-fated one. The superintendent and I had a nice conversation and lunched together, and he introduced me to a lot of people, both within the school system and in the community. Most importantly, the Iron Range schools amazed me. The faculty and administrators had decent salaries. The schools had great athletic fields. All of the schools had indoor swimming pools. The schools also appeared to have much labor support like custodians, secretaries, carpenters, and grounds people. This novice guy anxious for a job was indeed impressed.

It didn't take much consideration on my part when offered the position. The starting salary was $3,400. At that time, the starting salaries on the Iron Range were among the best in the state. I was absolutely elated. This job just had to be great compared to fleshing out mink pelts, making diesel oil filters, building silos, or sticking rear ends into Ford vehicles.

I was on my way to a teaching career. It would be a new adventure for me. I was sure that I would have fun, which was always one of the most important criterion in my decisions. I would experience a region of the state that I had previously known little about. Hunting and fishing activities would be superb. I would be able to begin paying off my loans. It was definitely a euphoric moment when I signed that contract.

Part II

A FLURRY OF FACULTY HANDBOOKS NOT READ

Chapter 7
The First Job: A Rookie at Work

I desperately needed to get myself from Winona to Keewatin for the opening teachers' workshop, which was scheduled for a Monday. However, a difficulty arose because I was playing baseball for Lewiston, Minnesota, and we had an important play-off game on the Sunday before this workshop. And of course, as luck would have it the game went long into late afternoon. Consequently, I didn't get out of town until evening with three hundred miles to travel. This workshop would be my first of an eventual fifty-some of them. As it turned out, I never enjoyed any of them, but this first workshop seemed important, and I didn't think I should be a no-show.

Extremely late that Sunday night, I arrived at Grand Rapids, Minnesota, a city only twenty-six miles from Keewatin. Being exhausted and with no place to lodge in Keewatin, I checked into a motel in Grand Rapids. All I knew about Grand Rapids was that it was the hometown of Judy Garland (Frances Gumm). Early the next morning, I headed out for Keewatin. I did make it to the meetings on time. After the workshop sessions, I began looking for a place to flop. Luckily, I found a room to rent from a recently widowed elderly lady, who also offered to do my laundry for a small charge. The next day I was now ready to begin what turned out to be a fifty-eight-year teaching career.

My academic workload consisted of a combination of physical education and general science classes. Five classes a day seemed overwhelming. Also, just about everyone on the faculty, except the industrial arts guy, dressed in suits, sport coats, and ties. This practice presented a major problem for me because my entire wardrobe could fit in one medium-sized dresser drawer and on two closet hangers. The other problem was learning and pronouncing the names of my students. Many of the names ended in "ich" and "ick" (Slavic), "ski" (Polish), "inenen" (Finnish), and with numerous vowels (Italian). Not a "Smith" or a "Green" or a "Jones" or a "Brown" could be found in any of my five classes. Two million Smiths in the United States, and I didn't have a single one in any class.

The beginning of my teaching career was not all bliss. After about two months, one of the students really irritated me. In a very no-nonsense way, I let go with a verbal blurt that went something like this: "Don't get wise, bubble eyes." I think that I had a firm grip on his shirt lapels at the same time. A serious problem ensued when the other students began calling the lad "bubble eyes." His parents marched up to the school one day, madder than hell. The principal, my immediate supervisor, beckoned me from the other end of a long hallway to come hither with his long index finger. I swear that he had an index finger ten to twelve inches long. I could plainly see it from one end of the long hallway to the other end. On the way to his office, not so pretty thoughts raced through my mind. Sure as heck I am going to be fired. After grilling me in front of the parents about what happened, I was asked to leave the office. My only defense at this interrogation was that I wanted to say something different to the student due to his misbehavior, but chose not to dip into that lower level of terminology in front of the other students.

The parents enrolled him in a school in a neighboring city. In those days, enrollment in a school outside your school district meant paying a hefty tuition. The parents were so angry that they didn't care about the additional expense. I felt that cleaning out my desk might be a good idea. Later that same day, the principal requested another visit to his office. I thought about going back to work at the Saint Paul Ford plant. I was good at sticking rear ends into Ford frames. And Big Ed, my work partner, didn't mind my potty mouth at all. Upon nervously entering the house of punishment, the principal shoved a piece of paper in front of me on his desk. He pointed out that it contained a list of names of other troublemakers in the school, and that I should work on them. I never looked at the piece of paper, but I don't think it was a list at all; just his way of indicating that things were all right—this time.

Keewatin was a relatively small community with a population of about 1,800. Everyone seemed to know everyone. And everyone seemed to know all about everyone, both in and out of school. Sometimes it seemed like everyone acted like they were on the school board. School business was everyone's business. With the exception of a few parents, most parents wanted good discipline in their school. Little doubt existed about my having discipline in my classes. However, the parents who accused me of throwing their son into the swimming pool got the wrong information from someone. Their sensitive, delicate child weighed at least 275 pounds, and I was not Clark Kent.

It was true, however, that one incident almost went too far. I firmly grabbed a student, probably a junior, by the back of his neck to get his attention for some well-needed understanding. He turned toward me and raised his fists into a boxing stance. When I was in high school, one of the seniors in my class clocked the male librarian for trying to discipline him. Of course, the student was expelled, but that poor librarian had a badly puffed face for more than a few days. I thought to myself that there is no way in hell that a student is going to plant one on me, whether it meant my job or not. I slowly and calmly took off my sport coat, folded it, set it aside, and confidently pointed out to the disgruntled student that I was pretty damn good in fisti- cuffs. He immediately dropped his combative stance and apologized. I patted him on the back and told him to forget that the incident ever happened. We actually interacted with each other in a friendly manner after that tense moment.

Word gets around quickly in a small school. One day the students in a study hall got out of hand. The home economics teacher was in charge, more accurately not in charge. She was a nice elderly lady and had no idea how to quell what was a near riot. The fairly large group of students was being boisterous, throwing crushed paper at each other like snowballs and rebelling against doing their homework. The prin- cipal came to my office and asked me to go into the study hall and restore order. I thought why me? The principal was the alpha wolf disciplinarian in the school. I entered the study hall, politely asked everyone to help pick up the paper scraps and other debris and to get back to work. No yelling or threatening took place; rather in a calm voice I just asked them to do it. Lo and behold they just did it.

Although there were a few incidences of severe adolescence regarding behavior, some of which have already been mentioned, the high school students seemed to be more mature than most. Many of the boys were big kids, and the seniors looked older than seven- teen and eighteen years old. During the spring of my first year on the Iron Range, I went to the state high school basketball tourna- ment in Minneapolis. The tourney was a traditional time when high school students from all over the state would flood to the Twin Cities, many of them seeking booze and wild parties. Consequently, bars had to be especially vigilant about not getting caught serving liquor to under-aged kids. Most bars would have a security person at the door checking everyone's identification card before they could enter. I was nearing twenty-three years old, and my driver's license indicated as much to the burly guy at the door when he demanded to see it. I sat down on a stool at the bar, looked to my right, and unbelievably, one of my senior students was sitting on a stool next to me sucking up a beer. I asked, "How did you get in here?" He answered that he just walked in. I continued, "Didn't the guy at the door ask for your proof of age card?" The student replied, "No. What's the problem?"

Except for ticking off a parent once in a while, I got along fine on the Iron Range. I loved their favorite foods, much of the tasty things new to me like different kinds of sausages, pastas, gnocchi, and pasties, the latter two I had never heard of before. The rangers tended to be loud, and some swore a lot. They definitely were my kind of people. They would give you crap and expect some back. I was good at that. They did not like wimps. They were good people who would give you the shirt off their back. At least they would spend their last dollar in order to buy you a beer. I would occasionally stop in the American Legion Club after school for a beer with the natives. Rather than criticizing me for being in the wrong place, they would criticize those teachers who wouldn't mix with them for a beer. They were hard-working fun-loving people.

Outside of the classroom, I tried to stay as active as possible. In the fall of that first academic year, I participated in the alumni versus high school football game, even though I wasn't an alumnus. Midway through the scrimmage, I got clobbered in the nose, hard enough to bring blood. Oh how the students and the high school team loved the trickling of blood onto my sweatshirt. And oh how embarrassing it was for me! I played college varsity football for four years at Winona State University, captained the team my senior year, and was an all-conference selection in the Minnesota State College League. And here I was bloodied and walking off the field in a stupid high school foot-ball scrimmage. During the winter, I played with the town basketball team, and we were very good. We played all over the Iron Range, and I got to know the area well. Bob Dylan (Hibbing native) was already playing the bars at that time, but I never ran into any of his gigs. In the summer, I played for the town baseball team. Some people just never grow up.

People in the communities where I have taught often complained about teachers having a three-month vacation every year. I always countered that it was a three-month layoff. I would gladly work twelve months a year for a salary that was 12/9 times larger than the one I was being paid. The math was tough for a few of them to comprehend. Salaries in my early days of teaching never placed me in the upper tax brackets, and many of us had to find summer employment for survival. Sometimes we even did part-time work during the school year.

While teaching on the Minnesota Iron Range, working in the mines during the summer months was an excellent opportunity to make some extra dollars. I was given a lot of different jobs in the mines because for the most of the summer I was replacing other workers who went on vacation. I liked that situation because the job was different every few weeks. Some of these jobs were a lark, and others were extremely hard labor. As a teacher working in the mines, many of the regular miners thought that I might be a marshmallow. So I had to always prove that I was not a marshmallow.

I started as a dump man on the brutal night shift. I really hated that job. A dump man was stationed on top of a large hill of rock and taconite (called a dump), that is, material stripped from the open pit mine. Huge Euclid trucks would come up to the top of the dump with loads of more rock and taconite. I had to signal where to back up with a large flashlight in the pitch-black night and make sure that they came as close as possible to the edge of the dump. If I stopped the driver and the truck too soon, the load would end up on the top of the dump rather than going over the edge. When the rock built up on the edge of the dump, the foreman would give you hell. If I allowed the trucks to back up too far, the truck and its driver would risk going over the edge. In this case, we were flirting with the possibility of a dangerous situation, and the foreman would surely give you hell. Such disasters had happened in previous years resulting in truck driver deaths, and I was constantly worried about causing another such mishap.

Pulling cable was a messy, beastly job. When the massive shovels had to be moved in the bottom of the pit, several of us bottom of the totem pole flunkies were recruited to pull the heavy rubber-coated electrical cable along with the moving shovel. Most often the mine pit was a big bowl of sticky muck. The job was a heave-ho activity in a foot of mud. But even a marshmallow was capable of handling other jobs in the mines. Being the railroad-crossing guy was boring. I would spend all day sitting on a big rock by the railroad tracks. If a train happened to come by, I would have to hold up my hand and stop any of those big Euclid trucks should they happen to come by at the same time as a train. The meeting of the two giant machines only happened once during the entire eight-hour shift. I did, however, become very good at hitting trees with pebbles.

Shovel oiler was another sweet job. About fifteen minutes before the start of the shift, I would have to crawl up the boom on the monstrous shovel and squirt oil and grease here and there. Then I had nothing else to do until the shovel operator stopped for a lunch break. This lunch break meant another hectic fifteen minutes in which I had to work my tail off squirting oil and grease here and there. Then I would wait for the end of the eight-hour shift so I could go home. I got a lot of magazines read while on this job.

I liked being a mechanic's helper. Most of time I stood around watching the head mechanic watching big water pumps, which were used to push the water out of the bottom of the pits. Sometimes I had to hand him a screwdriver or pliers. I was kind of like a mechanic's nurse. Once, however, we had to install a new pump on a raft-like platform situated in the middle of a large pond of water in the bottom of the mine. Electric cable needed to be transported to the pump on the platform. I stood in a not very big rowboat along the shoreline as a huge crane lifted a large roll of the heavy-coated cable and lowered it toward me in the rowboat. I was positive that the massive cable would be too heavy for the dinky boat, and I expressed this feeling to the boss guys on shore. But what the heck does a schoolteacher know? So they lowered the cable into the boat in which I was standing on one end. The boat, the cable, and the schoolteacher immediately underwent a smooth descent straight down to the bottom of the pond. As the water slowly rose above my head, I left one arm above the water so that I could wave bye-bye to the mental giants on shore. Thankfully, the water wasn't any deeper than my height plus the length of one raised arm, and I was only about twenty feet from the shoreline. I simply walked back to the shore. Even the foreman got a good laugh from it, and he never laughed.

The most exciting job I had was dynamiter's helper. After deep holes were drilled into the rock in the bowels of the mine, we would fill the holes with huge sticks of dynamite (very huge) and carefully pack the hole with surrounding soil. Then a loud siren would blare, and a flag would be raised on the top edge of the mine warning everyone to get the heck out of the mine before we blasted. Everyone would clear out of the mine pit except for the head dynamiter and the schoolteacher. The two of us would crawl under one of those big Euclid trucks. The dynamiter said it was safe under the truck because the rocks "should" go straight up. When the rocks come back to earth, the truck would act as an impenetrable shield. My immediate question was what if the rocks go horizontally? He explained that the set up shouldn't explode horizontally if we prepared the holes properly. Then he said push the plunger. Thankfully for my wife, my future children, and me, our dynamiting skills worked perfectly every time. The rock raining down on the truck was extremely loud and a bit of a rush. This job certainly increased the rate of one's heartbeat.

Keewatin was not only the beginning of my professional career, but also the beginning of my married life. I met the love of my life in Keewatin, and we married after my second year of teaching at the high school. My bride and I decided to splurge on a two-week honeymoon in the Dakotas, Wyoming, and Colorado. The plan was to have a good time and blow what little money we had. I would resume work in the mines when we got back until the start of the school year. It seemed like a good plan except when we returned the mining workers were involved in a strike and the mines were completely shut down. We were so broke that I thought I was back in college. We somehow managed to barely get through the summer. I worked behind a meat counter in a local grocery store and did some street maintenance work for the city. What a great way to start a marriage!

My father-in-law further increased my love for hunting and fishing, and therefore, my outdoor activity also greatly increased. He was a superb outdoorsman, and because of him, I experienced much of Minnesota's north woods and many of its famous lakes. We found ourselves in the wild during many weekends. One day, however, we simply went for a drive, and we stopped in Deer River, Minnesota, for a beer. After being served our beer at a table, I asked the bartender about several pools of blood that were on the floor. In a matter of fact way, he told us that the two guys standing at the bar beat up a Native American, and the bloodied victim went for help. That served beer was consumed nonstop in world-record time, and we were out of there in several nanoseconds.

As much as I liked the Iron Range, the urge to move on persisted. A couple of good reasons kept gnawing away at me. One important factor was the distance to the Twin Cities. A four-hour drive kept one from visiting the bright lights of Minneapolis very often. And then there were the tundra-like temperatures that descended upon the region much of the winter. One winter resulted in temperatures as low as -40°F, and more than -50°F not too far away (ironically in Cotton, Minnesota). I don't think that the temperature ever reached above zero during all of January one winter, even at high noon. I didn't have access to a garage so I would run the car hard to warm it up at 11 or 12 o'clock at night and then tuck in the engine under the hood with an old heavy army blanket. Then early in the morning, I would remove the blanket, start the car, and run it some more before heading out to work. One morning, I forgot about the blanket before starting the car.

A major league entanglement between the blanket and the engine's fan resulted. That did it. I was going to migrate south, at least farther south in Minnesota. Not much later in the spring, I resigned and activated my vitae. Resigning from one position before having locked in on another position was really a stupid move. But hey, everyone will probably want my services. I'm an experienced teacher now.

I spent three years on the Iron Range, and the experience had been great. But I now needed to find another job. Sammy's Pizza was started in neighboring Hibbing, Minnesota while I was teaching in Keewatin. The pizza became well known in the Midwest, and Sammy developed a chain of pizza restaurants in about twenty-five cities in Minnesota, Wisconsin, and the Dakotas. One day, Sammy, the pizza giant who was a Keewatin native, asked if I would manage one of his restaurants. He offered to pay me $400 per month and 49 percent of the net profits. I distinctly remember these numbers because at that time it was a darn good financial offer. I am not sure whether he was serious because the proposition was made in a bar. At any rate, I responded: "Sammy, I do love your pizza, and I like money, but I have to teach."

Chapter 8
From the Iron Range to Agriculture

I was stupid. I resigned from my job on the Iron Range before I secured another position. Very late in the evening of June 15, 1957, my wife gave birth to our first child. At noon the next day, I had an appointment in a hotel lobby in downtown Minneapolis 185 miles away to interview for a teaching position in Spring Valley, Minnesota. Tired, blurry-eyed, and unshaven, I made it to the appointment on time (reminiscent of the movie *The Out of Towners*). Broke, out of work, and starting a family prompted me to consider taking the job even if the workload included washing dishes after hot lunch. Besides, this location in agricultural country was also fairly good pheasant-hunting territory. During the two days off for the Minnesota Education Association convention, which I never attended, I would be able to go pheasant hunting. I got the job, and in late summer of that year we loaded a small U-Haul trailer and the backseat of our beat up Ford with all of our worldly possessions and headed south. I remember warming the baby's bottle of formula on the hot radiator of the car along a highway somewhere near Rochester, Minnesota. Having already begun a teaching career on the Iron Range, this position would be a new challenge for me in farmland, and I was looking forward to it.

One of the first challenges I dealt with was buying beer. In this community, teachers didn't dare go into the municipal liquor store. The stalwart educators had to go to a neighboring community to buy their cases of beer hoping that no one would recognize them. I wasn't going to take such nonsense anymore, and I finally set a precedent. I went into the forbidden local municipal liquor store to buy a case of off-sale beer. One parent did ask me what I was doing in there because of the example that I should be setting for his son and other young people. I asked him what he was doing in there because as a parent I assumed that he would be closer to his son than me. He took the give-and-take discussion quite well, and later this parent, a car dealer, sold me a used Oldsmobile at a great price. His sons who I had in class now have huge car dealerships. Evidently, having a teacher who purchased his beer in the same town in which he taught school didn't wreck their lives.

I heard of a teacher who had a great technique to get the students' attention relative to establishing discipline. On the first day of class, he would come to the classroom early before any students were in the room, place a metal wastebasket in the doorway, and then leave. On the first day of classes, students are very apprehensive and they do not touch anything. Hence, the basket would still be there when the teacher arrived to start the class. He would then shout, "Who in the heck put that basket in the doorway?" With that outburst, he would kick the metal basket so that it would go flying into the wall across the room, making a tremendous noise. Picking the basket up, he would tell the class exactly where it was to be placed. Then he would start his class. He had no disciplinary problems for a long, long time.

I had a similar but spontaneous episode the very first day that worked out quite well for me at the new school. I was in charge of a study hall with at least fifty or sixty students in it. I had sheets of paper circulating down each row of desks so that I could make out a seating chart. As I walked between two rows of desks supervising the task, one student began screwing around with another student across the aisle. I came from behind and politely placed his arm back on his own desk. He looked up at me and began to say "Watch that . . . ," and I impulsively whipped around and *accidently* backhanded him. He fell out of his desk flat on his back on the floor between two rows of desks. The fall was due to a combination of a push, some shock, and then gravity. Nonetheless, there he was lying on the floor looking at the ceiling without bending his neck. I leaned over him and asked whether he was about to say something. He said no, and I allowed him to get up and return to his desk. It was a great start for the first day. The discipline thing was established. The call went out. Be careful of the madman who had just arrived from the Iron Range.

The first principal whose drums I had to march to at this school was an okay person, but he was strictly education 101. Everything had to be done by the 101 book, probably the faculty handbook. I never got around to reading that book. For example, he absolutely insisted that we do lesson plans each week and turn them in to him. I always argued that the effort was a waste of time. He argued that these plans were important. I argued that lesson plans left little room for creativity, spontaneity, and improvisation. He argued that we should always know exactly what we are doing on any given day. I argued that they were never read by anyone. He asserted that lesson plans were indeed read every week—by him. So it was time for an experiment. I dutifully turned in my lesson plans each week. On Monday, we will go to the park and feed corn to the pigeons. On Tuesday, we will go to the pool hall and learn how to shoot snooker. On Wednesday, we will just sit around and tell dirty stories, and so forth. Three or four months lapsed before the principal noticed that some of my lesson plans displayed a case of near insubordination, and therefore, we had another discussion. I liked my teaching job, and I quickly gave in to authority. A friend of mine who was teaching industrial arts at another school went through a similar scenario. He and his principal engaged in their argument via notes being exchanged in their postal boxes at the school. Finally the exasperated principal placed a note in my friend's box asking, "George, you wouldn't build a house without a plan, would you?" George returned the note with a simple response, "I did." And indeed George actually did that.

Lesson plans were the least of my troublesome antics. A more serious reaction to a circumstance occurred within my first month on this new job. The school had a split noon hour meaning that some students were on lunch break while others were in classes. This kind of schedule meant that the halls had to be kept quiet. I had hall duty on the second floor, and I thought that things were pretty darn orderly.

A ninth grade math teacher had his classroom on the second floor near the top of the stairs. This guy's class was a circus—sheer mayhem. He had no control over his students. In spite of his inept attempt to be in control, he stormed out of his classroom one day and began barking at me for not keeping the hallway quiet. Seriously, I thought that his class was disturbing the halls. It was so ridiculous and I was so dumbfounded that I didn't know how to respond. So without thinking I impulsively asked him how he would like to be thrown down the stairs. Of course, he relayed the encounter to the principal, and once again I was in trouble. I was told that professionals do not handle differences by threatening to throw their colleagues down the stairs. I weathered this latest storm, and Mr. Ninth Grade Math Teacher was fired before the Christmas break of that first year.

Mr. Education 101 came up with an idea: every week or two the entire high school faculty would meet and the teachers would take turns in leading a discussion on some facet of education. When it was my turn, I surveyed a number of the faculty with regard to how they graded their students, and then I reported the information to the group. Frankly, I was astonished by some of the ways that some teachers actually graded. Grades were given for such superfluous things like adjusting the shades, straightening the classroom, and good behavior. I kept everything anonymous, and I ridiculed some of the practices. The session definitely disturbed some of the teachers. I guess it was the science in me in which we tend to grade on what the student learns, what the student comprehends, and how the student solves problems, communicates answers, thinks through various relationships, and makes applications. Nonetheless, my sarcasm showed through. I realized that everyone's efforts should be respected. But this was not the only blatant goof in my teaching career.

The innovative principal never ran out of educational gems. He placed a suggestion box in the hallway for students to come up with ways to improve the school. On the surface, the idea didn't sound too bad. The very first suggestion that he pulled out of the box went something like the following: "Some girls in this school do not know how to f——. I think that there should be a course to teach the girls how to do it. This course would make the school much better." The suggestion box was immediately terminated.

I found that I was capable of making my share of miscues, both in and out of the classroom. One of the best was when I was going to show the class how a distiller system worked. To do this demonstration, I needed cool water running through the distillation jacket. For some reason, the water from the faucet in my classroom was too warm. So I ran a hose from the distillation apparatus all the way through a preparation room into the adjacent chemistry lab where I hooked the hose up to that faucet. After explaining the concept of distillation to my class, I went into the chemistry lab to turn on the faucet. Upon doing so, I could immediately hear loud screaming. The hose had blown off the distiller in my classroom, and it was waffling back and forth spraying the entire class. Consequently I rushed back into my classroom and made a sharp kink in the hose with my hands to stop the flow of water and the community shower. When I bent the hose the back pressure blew off the hose connection on the faucet in the chemistry lab and sprayed the first couple rows of the class in that room! The principal heard the screams, came running down the hall, and just rolled his eyes.

Some mistakes were more dangerous. One such case was the self-made hydrogen bomb. I was showing the class how to make hydrogen, and I had the generating bottle set up with all of the necessary ingredients ready to make this highly explosive gas. Luckily, I decided that it might be a good idea to wrap the hydrogen-generating bottle with a towel and bind it with twine. The demonstration went well. I generated hydrogen in a bottle so we could place glowing splinters into the bottle and watch the wood burst into flames with a loud popping-like noise.

But then I had to get fancy. I was going to demonstrate how a gas jet works by applying a match to the glass tubing coming out of the hydrogen-generating bottle. The entire apparatus exploded. Due to the towel that I had wrapped around the bottle for safety purposes, the pieces of the apparatus went straight up, past my nose by a few inches, and through the ceiling tile with a tremendous crash. Seconds later, small pieces of glass rained down from the ceiling. The opening on the glass tubing was obviously too large, causing a good mixture of hydrogen and air, a serious combination. The principal frantically ran down the hall to my lab. I calmly asked him "What?" We were just conducting a little demonstration. He looked at the shattered glass on the floor and rolled his eyes.

The frog incident was just plain funny. I was going to demonstrate the conduction of an impulse in the big sciatic nerve that runs into the hind leg of a frog. First I pithed a frog by running a sharp needle into its brain. However, I didn't send the probe down the frog's spinal cord to remove all of the reflex action. After dissection to expose the large sciatic nerve, I was going to cut out a short length of it for our experiment. I was holding the dangling brain-dead frog as I attempted to cut the nerve. That proved to be quite a stimulus, and the *dead* frog *leaped* out of my left hand into the lap of a nice shy girl in the front row. More screams! And the principal walked by rolling his eyes.

Some administrators liked to separate students into class sections based on their academic ability in order to make the classes more homogeneous. I was not fond of placing students into pigeon holes based on their abilities. I always thought that the lower ability students could learn something from the higher ability students and that maybe the higher ability students could even learn something from the lower ability students. Being together and helping each other might be good for both types of students. Another counterproductive outcome is that some students in the lower tier often tend to be disruptive when together, sometimes emerging into real disciplinary problems. Because such a class was rather homogeneous, students learned a lot of disruptive behavior from each other and tried to outdo each other with their stupid antics. In addition, I thought that these students knew exactly why they were placed into the so-called lower group, and therefore, many of them didn't think that they could do any good class work. Basically, they were stigmatized.

Many students in the lower tier classes of secondary school certainly needed special help. My teaching load at the new job in Spring Valley included one such group in junior high, assigned to me to teach a general science course. I didn't have to be an educational giant to quickly realize that a big factor in their poor academic results was their inability to read well, or at all. In a bold move, I took the textbooks away from them. They couldn't read the books with any kind of comprehension anyway. Hence, I conducted a science demonstration for them almost every class period. Following the fun part, we would delve into the science underlying the demonstration. I could immediately tell that the students' curiosity was much better than their reading ability, and they loved the procedure. I also sensed that their capacity to think was not nearly as bad as others had assumed. Standing on my head drinking a glass of water thrilled them, and they learned all about peristaltic action. I demonstrated that a dropped softball from the roof of the school building would indeed hit the ground at the same time as the softball thrown horizontally from the roof. I darn near fell off the roof throwing the ball. And they learned some rudimentary physics. I showed them that a 12-pound shot put and a softball would hit the ground at the same time when dropped together. More physics! I was just as surprised as the students that these experiments actually worked. When the principal saw me on the roof of the school building, and all those kids out on the school grounds watching the bizarre proceedings, I am sure that he was once again rolling his eyes. By now he must have been getting very good at rolling his eyes.

I set up a demonstration whereby when I spit into a metal container the ingredients within it would burst into flames. This shocking result led to a neat discussion of elementary chemistry. Another fun thing was to have a female student kiss the surface of some agar medium in a Petri dish. After a couple of days, an imprint of her lips was well defined in a bacterial outline on the agar surface. Dates came hard for her following that experiment. I also set up a demonstration before class in which I would place a small beaker into a larger beaker holding a specific mixture of liquids. The liquid mixture had exactly the same refractive index properties of glass; hence, one couldn't see the small beaker in the larger beaker. Then during a fake demonstration, I would *accidentally* break a beaker of the same size and shape as the one already placed in the large beaker. Students always loved it when the teacher broke something. After pointing out that it was no big deal, I would pick up the pieces of glass, throw them into the large beaker, perform some magic hand movements, utter dumb magic words, and pull out an unbroken beaker. More interesting science discussion followed.

One other trick that I really liked almost backfired. I wet my arm with a colorless solution before the class arrived. A different colorless solution was smeared on a large butcher knife. I would start the class by pointing out that I was going to dissect something, like a cow heart. With a quick stroke, I would rub the back edge of the knife across my lower arm to bring the two colorless solutions together. This maneuver was, of course, another *accident*. The two solutions together turned into an instantaneous blood red color. Then I would go into an act of extreme pain. A timid little girl in the front row began to look pale, and I thought that she was about to topple over. Rapidly cleaning my arm with paper towels and imploring her to understand that the whole thing was a joke slowly stabilized her. But it wasn't just a joke. The class learned some more basic chemistry from Mr. Fool Around.

My favorite asinine fooling around stunt was the candle episode. Before class, I built what looked like a candle out of a short piece of ripe banana by rubbing it into a smooth appearance and placing it in a real candlestick holder with wax dripping. It was a very convincing production. A sliver of a pecan, very high in lipid (fat) content, worked nicely for a wick. When the class assembled, I pretended to do a demonstration of some kind, and I lit my fake candle that actually burned. Then I pointed out that instead of the demonstration I was going to eat the *candle* because I was very hungry. With that I snuffed out the flame and tossed the candle into my mouth. As I proceeded to chew the candle, only a few students laughed or even snickered. Most students just sat there in disbelief. I did notice one student in the back row swirling his hand around his ear, a symbolic motion indicating that the teacher is crazy. I wanted to discuss lipid content in nuts with the class, but no one asked about how I could eat a candle; hence, I never told them. I sometimes wonder about their class reunions.

I could always get help from certain students to pull off other capers. For example, I convinced one student to have him in the act of shooting a spitball at exactly 11:23 on the big clock in the front of the room. At this specific time, I would have my back to the class while writing on the board. At that precise second, I would yell, "Charlie, put down that spitball."

When discussing mental telepathy with them, I would look up their records in the office ahead of time. Then I would intensely concentrate on their thoughts and blurt out their birthday or something. Some never realized that I cheated, so in the interest of science

I would eventually tell them. And some of these students also had a sense of humor. One student, normally very quiet and not the swiftest kid, came up to me holding a small snuffbox. He claimed that he had caught a white bee, and that it was in the box. Considering my already blossoming genetic interest, the possibility of an albino bee really got me excited. This bee might be the result of an extremely rare mutation. Upon slowly and carefully opening the box, I found the letter "B" cut out of white typing paper. The tide had turned and the joke was on me. And it was a splendid show perpetrated by the quiet kid in the back row. He certainly deserved an "A" grade for creativity.

A problem with lower tier classes is that they can sometimes breed troublemakers. In my experience, it was not as apt to happen in classes consisting of students with mixed academic abilities. Lower tier students in lower tier classes try to be king of the hill in any way possible, even by bad behavior. I had one such student, an eighth or ninth grader, who was a real pain in the butt. Nothing reasonable to get him into line seemed to work, and I just couldn't take it any longer. He was not particularly big, and I finally grabbed him by the collar on the back of his shirt with one hand and the seat of his pants with my other hand. Down the hall we went, at least two hundred feet, and I don't think that his feet touched the floor more than a few times the entire trip. When we reached the outside door, I threw him out of the building and told him to go stand around on the streets. About two days later, the principal called me into his office. The principal explained to me in a matter of fact way that I had no right to kick a student out of school. Only the school board could take such a drastic action. I knew that such a situation must exist in the faculty handbook, but I acted dumb. He said that the student hung out in the washroom during my class, and that I had to allow him to return to the class. I did, and the student and I got along very well the rest of the year. It was another good ending.

Eventually I did have some actual face-to-face interaction with the school board. While on the faculty in this school district, I had the opportunity to be on the salary committee. It was a lot like the Democrats and the Republicans debating issues. A few of the meetings got a bit nasty. Of course to be fair, the board members had to be cognizant of their working budget and available revenue. But the argument that they used in an effort to keep salaries down, or at least in check, was to compare our salaries to every other little school district in the area. The counter argument made by the salary committee was that possibly this faculty was very good and that the district should want to keep them. The argument fell on deaf ears. One board member, a farmer, pointed out that lately he only made $4,000 a year. Upon pressing him with pointed questions, it was revealed that $4,000 was the amount that he saved after absolutely all of his farming and living expenses. No one on the faculty could save $4,000 a year when their salary was about $5,000 a year. We were told to live within our means. One teacher on the committee shouted, "I'll be damned if I will live within my means." Despite the humor in this comment, no one on either side laughed. I asked the board chairperson if the salary offer by the board was the last dictated negotiated offer. The chairperson slammed his notebook shut and loudly blurted out "Yes." I thought that the meeting went fairly well. We succeeded in ticking off absolutely everyone.

I thought the faculty was excellent, but some ugly attitudes always existed. I never turned to the administrators with any problems. I just took on handling everything myself. In fact, the second principal during my tenure at this school stated that if everyone conducted things like I did, there would be no need for a principal. However, I think he forgot the many times he had to call me into the office for handling things by myself. Nonetheless, I took his comment as a compliment. The faculty strangely consisted of several good teachers whose names all ended in "off." For example, there was "P—toff" and "K—koff." We added another guy with a persecution complex to the "off" group. We named him "Pissed off." Notwithstanding a few chronic complainers, most of the faculty was made up of very good teachers, and I never understood why they always voted against a merit pay system whenever such a vote came up. The vote always turned out to be about sixty against and only two for a merit system. The two nonconformists were a mathematics teacher and myself.

Regardless of the many out-of-the-classroom episodes, which I did not always relish, I really enjoyed teaching biology at this school, so much that on many days I could hardly wait to get into the classroom. Field trips were a blast except for the time a herd of perturbed cows (with calves) chased us out of a field (we all made it). Or the time we nearly walked through a patch of poison ivy (I detected the plants just in time). I also enjoyed teaching the biology students in the laboratory. I had excellent lab facilities, and we conducted numerous experiments and projects. Still I did not get involved in science fairs. I always felt the award system was greatly unfair because of the difficulty in judging the extensive help from their teachers, parents, and other professional acquaintances. I recall a teacher at another school who decided that all of his students would do a project and that the preparation for the science fair would be completely left up to the students. After some time, very few students had a project of their own, and they were becoming restless. To quell their whining, he angrily blurted out that they should simply do anything—build a fire extinguisher or something. The students in his class turned in twenty fire extinguishers for their projects. Heck, even university graduate students rarely know what to research on their own.

A bold and interesting adventure during my tenure at this school was chaperoning sixty-five senior students to Washington, D.C., for a week along with my wife and one other teacher and his wife. We told the students that if they created any trouble they were to call their parents and leave us out of it. Laying down the law worked quite well, although I found out later that the students built a pyramid out of empty beer cans in one of the hotel rooms, close to the size of those in Egypt. I think that those sixty-five students were more concerned about their four chaperons behaving well than we were about them.

An interesting event occurred on the visit to the US Capitol Building. The group was supposed to meet with Senator Hubert Humphrey. The time period was during the Johnson administration, and at that time Senator Humphrey was an important leader in the senate. While waiting to meet with Senator Humphrey, his aids informed us that he had just arrived from the state of Washington and was immediately called to the White House for an urgent meeting with President Johnson. Senator Humphrey's aids, however, were instructed to hang on to these students until he could get to the Capitol. So the Humphrey aids discussed some mundane governmental topics while our hung-over students mostly snoozed while sitting on the floor in a hallway. These tired, red-eyed, future leaders of America couldn't have cared less about the workings of the government. Eventually, Senator Humphrey arrived and he immediately broke into a moving talk about how things work in Washington, D.C., and world politics. The students rose from the dead and dwelled on his every word. He had them in the palm of his hand. After he finished, I heartily thanked him and pointed out that his effort was beyond the call of duty considering how busy he was with national concerns. Besides I said, most of these kids were probably Republicans. Senator Humphrey responded in his usual head nodding emphatic way, "That is why I needed to talk to them." A couple of weeks later, I received a letter from Mr. Humphrey thanking us for staying at the Capitol until he could meet with the students. Truly amazing!

After a teacher has gained some experience in the profession, personnel in colleges of the region often ask you to supervise teachers-to-be (practice teachers). I always took this supervision very seriously. It could make or break a person's intended career, which was quite a responsibility considering that I didn't even get paid for the extra task. The most serious problem some of these aspiring teachers had was that they attempted to be just like the supervisor. It simply does not work. I would always force my opinion on them that they should be their own person and develop their own style. Occasionally, it was blatantly obvious that a practice teacher might not make it in the real world of teaching. It was extremely difficult to be honest with an individual about such a situation, but very necessary. I thought that some of these individuals should try to become CEOs of a large company (one did), or sell cars, or take some more education courses and become a school administrator.

Teaching in a relatively small city requires more than just teaching. You are asked to be involved in everything, that is, everything from softball and baseball teams, to donkey basketball in order to make an ass out of yourself, to working bingo events, to church committees. As a teacher, your activity in everything is simply expected. For example, it was decided that a new church had to be built. Consequently many of the teachers who belonged to that parish were asked to be on the building committee and go around and ask people for money or pledges. I emphatically pointed out that this kind of activity was asking me to be someone I am not. But the clergy guy was persuasive, and I reluctantly agreed to give it a try. The very first house that I visited was the residence of a person who had a fine successful business. His house was large and evidently expensive. This family was not on food stamps. The ensuing discussion was one-sided in favor of the businessman who went on and on about how tough things were. Finally I decided to leave and when I reached the door, I pressed a dollar bill into his hand and left. I'll never forget the look on that guy's face. At the next meeting, I told the other committee members and the clergy guy that I quit the team. The drive for a new church had already cost me a dollar.

Just like being on the Iron Range, I had to again seek summer employment in Spring Valley. A local lumberyard company that also had a construction crew provided me with a chance to earn a few precious extra dollars. The boss guy always gave me the most dangerous and rotten jobs like painting a cupola on a mile-high barn, or making eave troughs work properly on a mile-high house, or pouring concrete with a wheelbarrow (at least I was on the ground for a change).

Once he sent a young college student and myself out to a farm to shingle a mile-high old house. This job wasn't unreasonable to accomplish because I had some shingling experience, until we encountered the bees living under the old wood shingles. These bees were an extremely angry territorial bunch. We tried every kind of spray known to mankind in an effort to get rid of them, but they just got more ticked at us. We even poured gasoline on them, but to no avail. I think that they went on a high with the gas and became even more erratic. Finally I developed a plan. I knew exactly where the bees were coming out of the old roof. So after they settled down, I sneaked up the roof with a hammer and an asphalt shingle with the intent to quickly entomb the damn beasts. With my heart racing, I nailed down the asphalt shingle over their opening as quickly as possible. Little did I know that the bees had a backdoor at another part of the roof. They took after the college guy who was standing on the ground. In sheer fright, he ran through the adjacent woods and thicket knocking down saplings and every bit of flora in his way. Luckily he only got stung once, but the swelling was a major league welt. Telling the boss that there was no way in hell we could shingle that house brought uncontrollable laughter from the old-timers on the construction crew. One of them confidently went out to the farm to finish the job. He was back within an hour with the same sorry story. That house could not be shingled until bee experts were hired to handle the bees with their special smoke bombs. By the way, the college guy who made a new path through the woods ended up playing outside linebacker for the New York Giants in the NFL. Evidently handling NFL ball carriers was a lot easier than dealing with those darn bees.

In addition to the egg-money income by pretending to be a carpenter, I became very interested in freelance photography. Good photography was like real science, and I loved it. Besides making a voluminous number of 35 mm transparencies for my biological teaching, I tried to make some money. I was not into portraits, family photos, weddings, babies, and so forth, although I did a little of that photography for a few friends. I was not good with people. I stuck with fruit flies, grasshoppers, and other biological subjects.

Trade magazines were my primary sources. For example, I sold a photograph to the American Nylon Association showing my students using women's nylon socks to filter plankton out of creek water. I sold a photograph of a mammoth tree gall to the Cleveland Tree Surgeon Company (the caption stated that I had a lot of gall). I sold a photograph of a massive field of turkeys to the American Turkey Association. I sold wild flowers to a greeting card company. I did close-up photography of teats on cows for a veterinarian researching various maladies of teats.

I won some photo contests using my kids as subjects. I developed a set of slides showing close-up views of weed and grain seeds that became a great hit with high school agricultural teachers. As a result of all these photographic activities, I probably added a couple of thousand dollars to the revenue side of our budget, not really a windfall. However, not bad for someone who got a "D" grade in the visual arts class in college. I got to thinking that I was pretty good, and I checked out a job for a photographer of a large industrial company in the Twin Cities. They were very interested in my taking the job. But once again I came back to my senses. I have to teach.

During the years in Spring Valley, children numbers two, three, four, and five were born. Birth number two (Greg) was an interesting situation. The nearest hospital was in Rochester, Minnesota, twenty-six miles away. Late one night, Greg was in a terrible hurry to enter the world, and we raced to the hospital at about ninety miles per hour, even passing a parked highway patrol car without waking the officer. I didn't know exactly where the hospital was located. Initially, we ended up at the mental institution. When finally getting to the correct hospital, little Greg already was nearly a legal tax deduction. Before I even signed the insurance forms, the nurse came by and told me it was a boy. Then the hospital had the audacity to charge me for the labor room, which obviously was not used. I balked on principles, and the hospital people and I traded arguments by mail for a couple of weeks; the situation was clearly an impasse. Finally, I told the hospital administrators that they would have to repossess the kid. Two days later, a new billing arrived with the labor room crossed out. The poor kid was stigmatized at the early age of three weeks.

I hated missing classes for any reason. I could always overcome my own illnesses and show up for my classes, but with five young children I often found myself in emergency rooms and hospitals. Consequently, I also found myself teaching with very little sleep on many occasions. One time I observed a social studies teacher fall asleep at the blackboard while teaching a class. He was leaning against the board talking to the class and off he went into a snooze. I later found out, however, that the little nap was not due to a late night sick child problem; rather, it was a late night on the town problem.

At the start of our decade-long stay in Spring Valley, we rented a very old house from two elderly sisters who moved to another community. We could only use the ground floor because the sisters stored several tons of their belongings in the upper floor, and it was off limits to us.

Soon thereafter using shoestring finances, we purchased a house toward the edge of town along a state highway. As novice homebuyers, this transaction constituted a number of mistakes: purchasing a house before we could actually afford it, buying a rambler-type house against our tastes, no available garage, and located on a well-traveled highway.

One morning I found a guy, well inebriated, sleeping in my car. After waking him and letting him know that he should get his butt out of there, I asked him about what he was celebrating. He flatly stated that his mother-in-law had died. On another occasion at about 2:00 a.m. on New Year's Eve, a very cold fellow, also inebriated, was pounding on our door. It was a very windy -20°F evening, and he was only wearing a small light jacket. He related how he was celebrating in a bar, decided to walk home, but found himself confused and hopelessly lost. I gave him a ride home (he knew his address) and strategically pointed out my name. Who knows? He might have been rich and placed me into his will. No money has come my way yet.

Sparky, a nearby neighbor, was also well known for overdoing alcohol consumption. He had a truck and evidently did livestock trading of some kind. To the town's people, he was legendary with regard to his ability to trade livestock. One story often floating around was that he got drunk and belligerent one night and ended up in jail in Preston, Minnesota, about sixteen miles from Spring Valley. The next morning, he was released with only a dollar or two in his pocket and without a vehicle. He began the journey home by walking and stopping at farms along the way. At one farm, he spent the little money he had to buy a chicken and then kept trading animals as he went from farm to farm. The punch line is that he ended up riding into town on a horse. True or not, it certainly sounded like our neighbor, Sparky.

Our third and last house in Spring Valley, also purchased on shoestring finances, was a large two-story house on a nice quiet residential street. Shortly after moving into this swell roomy house, we sadly sold it and moved to the Twin Cities because I had another ambition, that is, resident graduate school and a Ph.D.

Spring Valley was a great proving ground. I learned important things like being on the good side of the secretaries, custodians, and hot lunch cooks. I purposefully left out administrators, but I did get along with them too. This was the school where I wrote and published my first article—in *The American Biology Teacher*. Spring Valley was where our family increased from one to five tax deductions. It was where my wife developed her interest in antiques, an interest that later developed into a business. It was a town where I could charge my groceries without a credit card. It was a town where I could get a bank loan with very little collateral when times were really tough (and that was often). It was a friendly town and leaving it was not easy.

Forty-five years since working in that town, I had a heart echo examination at Mayo Clinic in Rochester, Minnesota. The technician came into the lab, looked at my appointment sheet, and asked if I had ever lived and taught school in Spring Valley. After confirming that I was the guy, he said that he had heard my name many times because his older brother was on the same faculty with me. I asked why my name came up so often and whether the name was mentioned in a good or bad way. With much discretion, he related that he couldn't remember the details and quickly began the heart echo examination. Also after forty-five years, I still get invitations to attend class reunions at Spring Valley, and I usually go to them.

My wife and I had more than a few trepidations about chaperoning
sixty-five high school senior students to Washington, D.C., for an entire week.
These students, however, were well behaved beyond our expectations.
I am second from the right in the front row, and my wife, Rose, is standing
in the far left of the top row.

Two of the students were excited to converse with Minnesota's favorite son, Senator Hubert Humphrey. The senator had just finished a sterling talk to the high school group of students, claiming that he had to speak to them because some of the students were probably Republicans.

Chapter 9

Two Master's Degrees While Teaching

Ever since undergraduate college years, I had seriously thought about obtaining a doctorate degree someday. But obstacles always existed. Firstly while in college, I never had appropriate counseling in this regard. I didn't have the slightest idea about how graduate school worked, that is, the availability of assistantships, testing procedures, applications, and so forth. Also, when you come out of college with a massive debt of about $2,400, you have to immediately go to work. In those days $2,400 was a rather substantial amount of money. Then during that first position, one can fall in love and have children, all of which leads to debt that makes the $2,400 debt seem miniscule. Eventually you get so mired down in your present job that standing on your head while drinking a glass of water in teaching general science classes may be your ultimate fate. However, demonstrating peristaltic action to those students was just as important as other academic endeavors.

On October 4, 1957, the Russians sent *Sputnik I* into space, and science in this country underwent many progressive changes. How could the Russians beat the United States into space? The outcry was that science had to improve, and the National Science Foundation became the recipient of a lot of dollars legislated by the U.S. Congress. One of their many ideas was a program geared to send high school science teachers back to college during the summer months in order to update their science skills. To entice teachers away from working in lumberyards and shingling bee-infested houses during the summer, tuition was free and stipends for living expenses were even paid. The amount of the stipend was proportional to the size of your family. The money was much better than one could get from working in lumberyards. In addition, participants could pick up a few graduate credits for possible transfer some day to an actual graduate degree program. One of the downsides included being away from your home and family and living in dormitories or taking the family with you and living a Spartan life in small, grungy, hot rentals without air-conditioning.

I took advantage of several of these programs. The University of South Dakota in Vermillion on the banks of the Missouri River was as much humidity as I had ever experienced. Although I never missed a class, I also spent a lot of time playing intramural softball, and my biggest accomplishment during the summer was being named to the all-star team. The science program at Iowa State University in Ames was okay, but at that time you couldn't even buy a cocktail anywhere in that damn town. Didn't they know that the Prohibition Act was repealed in 1933?

The University of Minnesota program was kind of fun because it was held at their Itasca Biological Station in northern Minnesota. However, the mosquitoes were plentiful and were the size of hummingbirds. Removing wood ticks from your body was a daily ritual. Field trips through the bogs were also very exciting. Every once in a while as we ploughed through the bog in single file someone would nearly disappear. Some of those bogs were simply a thin layer of land covering a very deep body of water. A person could go through the thin layer of land into the deep water. Thankfully, we never permanently lost anyone. In addition to learning some biology at the government's expense, the fishing in Lake Itasca was great.

This National Science Foundation program at the University of Minnesota Itasca Station was designed for teachers with good laboratory skills in biology, but maybe too weak in the ecological areas. Twenty-five teachers from across the country and myself supposedly fit this mold, although I felt rather confident and adept in the woods. To conduct a research project, I was paired with a guy from Baltimore, Maryland, who I thought had never before been in the woods. Everything scared the heck out of him, from mosquitoes to deer.

The two of us were assigned to do some kind of a transect through the woods measuring the circumference of trees. I have never been sure why we were asked to measure those trees. We were mostly clueless and were given minimal directions. But I did my homework, studied maps of the area, and came to the godsend realization that Douglas Lodge (a rather famous resort) was not too far away in a particular direction from the biology station. This information was used to exactly plan the route (transect) through the woods with an ulterior motive. The placement of the route was supposed to be chosen randomly, but I hedged a little (actually a lot). By carefully following my calculations, the Baltimore guy and I trekked through the woods and came upon this oasis in the north woods. After a few martinis by poolside, we would head back to the biology station. Everyone thought that we were putting in very long hours in the woods measuring the circumference of trees. I hate to brag, but this caper was one of my best.

One participant in this National Science Foundation program who was from somewhere in Illinois really got under my skin for a lot of reasons. Like always, I tried hard to make new friends, but it wasn't working. One of the visiting scientists to speak to the group was a geneticist. The central theme of his talk concerned severely mentally challenged individuals due to genetic causes. He closed his talk with some parting comments that included a rhetorical question. These genetic syndromes are severe, and no cure exists for them. So he asked, what can we do about these unfortunate people? I suggested that we allow them to teach high school in Illinois. The guy from Illinois went ballistic and fisticuffs seemed eminent. The confrontation turned out to be only verbal blather, and luckily for at least one of us, and maybe both of us, things didn't get physical. It was evident that not everyone enjoyed my warped sense of humor. Later that summer, I ran into the short-tempered one in a bar one night in Bagley, Minnesota, not far from the biology station. After a few tense moments, we half-heartedly made up and had a few beers together. Beer to the rescue again!

With Spring Valley only sixty miles from Winona State University, I also began working on a master's degree in education. Most of the people in the program had their sights set on school administration–type positions, but not me. I definitely wanted to continue teaching. Most of the time, I found teaching to be a great deal of fun. One of my professors advised me to take the GRE in education and maybe go after a Ph.D. in that field. I wasn't at all interested, but I took the test for the heck of it. Many of the questions were based on situations. I answered them completely opposite of what I would *really* do, and I received an extremely high score. Conventional educational protocol and my thinking about how to handle situations were evidently light years apart from each other. But the high score on the education exam was not important to me because that wasn't the area I wanted to enter anyway.

This master's degree program required a research project and a thesis. Because I was so good at finding resorts in the woods when at the University of Minnesota Itasca Station, I decided to conduct a plant taxonomic study. The proposal was accepted, and I went off into the woods every weekend. The objective of this project was to identify tree distributions at certain points across a three-county area, spanning a flatland county to a woodland type county with a flatland to woodland county of transition in between the other two counties. I thought that the study would be a lot of fun because I enjoyed tramping through the woods. But the real fun of doing this study had nothing to do with trees.

Parts of Houston County consist of rugged, forested, majestic hills. It was deep in these hills where I noticed a pair of beady eyes peering at me from the brush some distance away. After sending a warm hello to the wary one, he ran and I tentatively followed him. Coming across his little shack, I saw the same pair of beady eyes peering at me from a small window. I assumed that this hermit might get to town once in a while to buy shotgun shells. So I got the hell out of there.

On another occasion, a guy sneaked up on me. After restarting my heart and while explaining to him what I was doing, I could tell that this guy was also whacky. So I got the hell out of there.

On still another occasion, I walked out of the woods to find a guy attaching a log chain to the front bumper of my car. It was at the end of a narrow dirt road on the very top of a hill. I quickly grabbed some tree leaves and acted like I was some kind of an ecological big shot. I told him that I was with the State Department and asked him what the heck he thought he was doing. He was a religious freak thinking that a couple of lovers were probably in the woods doing it. He intended to pull my car down the hill with his Caterpillar. I wasted no time in getting the hell out of there. But the guy was not that far off base. Once I did come across a car parked exactly in the middle of the narrow country road with doors fully opened on both sides. They were indeed doing it. Realizing that this was a touchy event for the participants, I got the hell out of there.

Soon after getting this master's degree in education, I earned a second one, a master's degree in biology at Saint Mary's University of Minnesota. Armed with these two master's degrees, I thought that it might be the right time to make a run for the academic Holy Grail, the Ph.D. Based on my interests, genetics was the obvious choice to study and research. I liked biology, mathematics, statistics with its probability, and chemistry. Genetics seemed to be a combination of all these disciplines. Therefore, I took the necessary tests and was accepted to the University of Minnesota. However, by this time I wasn't able to begin graduate school residency until the following academic year. This posed no problem because I had already signed a contract to teach at Mounds View High School, a large Saint Paul suburban school.

The critical part of this grand plan was that I had to resign from my present position at Spring Valley. With two master's degrees and some significant longevity, I was probably one of the highest paid teachers in the entire school system. I had the security of tenure. We had four children and number five was on the way. We were in the process of buying a large house that we liked very much located in a nice neighborhood. Life was pretty good.

I discussed the details of this irrational plan with my wife. The details went something like the following. We were going to have to move to the Twin Cities. We would have to find another house, at Twin Cities prices. I was going to chase a Ph.D., meaning that it would take at least three or four years out of our lives. Financially, we would probably have to live like paupers. And there was no guarantee that I would successfully obtain the genetics degree. Genetics is a tough sport, and universities don't give these degrees away.

Absolutely everyone in our sphere of acquaintances thought that I had gone off the deep end. I wonder how many married individuals with five young children, who proposed to enter such an unpredictable situation, would still be married by the end of the week. Some of us are lucky to have exceptional wives.

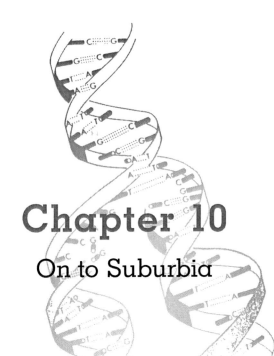

Chapter 10
On to Suburbia

I was actually getting wiser. This time I secured a new job before resigning from my present one. Previous to signing on at Mounds View High School, a Saint Paul suburban school, I had interviewed for a position at Lea College in Albert Lea, Minnesota, since only a master's degree was required. It was during the Vietnam War, and a lot of young people were entering college, some in order to stay out of the armed services. Lea College appeared to be a college put together precisely for that purpose. The dormitories were more like a country club than a college. But the classrooms were more like farming poultry buildings than a college. The educational system explained to me was very unorthodox. I thought that the college was bordering on being a farce, and I wanted no part of it. Of course, the college closed at the end of the war.

By the time I began teaching at Mounds View High School, I had already been accepted into graduate school at the University of Minnesota; consequently, I was sure that I would be at this new job for only one academic year. I thought it would be wise not to reveal this temporary employment situation until the time of resignation late in the year. I felt a little sneaky about my ultimate plan, but I had heard that all is fair in love, war, and clandestine educational matters. I had to revert to a lesser salary because the school district was not going to give me full credit for thirteen years of teaching experience. But my family and I would have an entire year to get moved and settled in the Twin Cities area. My grand plan was coming to fruition.

We settled into a house, which was much like a dollhouse compared to the one that we had left. It was located in a country setting just north of the Twin Cities. I liked the large tamarack swamp just beyond the backyard, but our closest neighbor family to the west of us was absolutely the pits. I called them the Jukes family. This neighboring family, of course, was not named Jukes. To put things into perspective, let me explain something about the real Jukes family. A researcher studied the Jukes family back in 1916 by tracing 2,096 members of this family over six generations. Their record of achievement was something to behold. Among the members traced, there were 140 hardened criminals, 7 murderers, 60 thieves, 300 sexually immoral individuals, 310 paupers, and 130 were guilty of other miscellaneous crimes. This neighbor clan was not that bad, but I still had reasons for calling them the Jukes family.

One day, we came home from a brief outing to find my sons' pellet rifle missing from the entryway. After many abrasive situations with this bunch (too many members in the family to get a good count), I couldn't take it anymore. I placed a hammer in my back pocket for a possible encounter with their vicious dog (dogs supposedly take on the personality of their owners) and headed for the neighboring house. A wire fence ran between the two properties, and I think that I went through it rather than climbing over it. The mother reluctantly answered the door. The dog was barking and growling while she was pleading the case that her kids were perfect. I sternly pointed out that they should put the dog in a safe place before I kill it and that her perfect kids should bring me the items that they had been stealing. After some bitter words and intense gnashing of teeth, one by one the neighbor kids began bringing me all kinds of items that they had pilfered. I wasn't aware that some of the items were even missing from our residence. I walked back to our house with my arms full of stolen goods.

The suburban school was big, much bigger than the previous schools where I had taught. In fact, the total of grades ten through twelve was almost four times larger than the population of my entire hometown. I never had much of a chance to know the administrators very well like I did at the other schools (probably a good thing). The school was so large, and I was so detached from how it worked that I sometimes thought I wouldn't even have to show up—no one would be aware of my absence, except maybe the teacher in the next room. The school district included families living in the suburbs of Arden Hills, New Brighton, and Mounds View, Minnesota, among a few others. I understood that the fairly new school and its name was a political move. Half of the large school building actually resided in Arden Hills, the other half was situated in New Brighton, and the school was named Mounds View. Probably great thinking went into settling various appeasements.

Mounds View High School was an interesting place. During the first conversation I had with the principal (probably the only one), I was informed about how exceptional the school and the students were and how I needed to be cognizant of this self-evaluated status when I did my grading. I didn't say it, but I was thinking that no one tells me how to grade my students. It turned out that the students came from a variety of domestic backgrounds like in most places. Some were poor, some were from broken homes, some were from extremely affluent families, and so forth. However, it did seem like most of the students had cars, and most of the cars were much nicer than my old beat up Chevy carryall. I recall getting a note from one of the mothers that was embroidered in gold lace of some sort. I guess that it was supposed to impress me. On the downside, I never experienced a worse hot lunch program. Most of the time, I couldn't determine what I was eating. I began carrying my own bag lunch.

My colleague biology teachers were good. However, they all seemed more interested in outdoor biology (ecological studies) than laboratory work. I liked outdoor field trips too, even taking my classes to a nearby swamp area to learn some ecology. And sometimes during my free period, I joined other biology classes and helped students with their tree identification. I knew the trees really well from past training and research. But I was also interested in conducting laboratory-type experiments. This objective posed a major problem because of a lack of instrumentation and glassware in the biology department. Butterfly nets, fish seines, hip boots, and plankton nets, however, were plentiful. In fact, I had to borrow a lot of laboratory materials from the chemistry department. I didn't bother creating any waves about what I perceived as a serious deficiency due to my short-term plans to stay at the school.

Still I have to admit that Mounds View was an excellent school in many ways, and most of the students were good students. Nonetheless, they also had lower tier classes, and the lucky new guy was assigned two such classes. And once again, I found myself trying to convince the students in these lower tier classes that they could indeed learn. But some students practically dared me to teach them. I took on their dare with vigor. I had always been able to maintain good discipline, but this time it was a greater challenge.

I was deemed the new guy from the small outstate school who thought he could rule the suburbanites. Also, times had changed. You were no longer allowed to lift a student off the floor by their lapels, put your nose in the kid's face, and have a serious discussion. I think that constituted illegally touching them. But I did it a few times anyway. You were no longer allowed to grab a mischievous kid by the back of the neck and seat of the pants and throw them out of the building. But I did it a couple of times anyway from the classroom to the hallway. It seemed that half of the students in one of my classes had parole officers, and they were proud of it. On a couple of occasions, I told a student to get the heck out of my classroom and go shoot the bull with your parole officer. The counselor would then inform me that I should have sent the student to them. One of the nemesis guys in class was the nephew of a person convicted as an accomplice in one of Minnesota's most infamous murders for hire. I tried to talk nice to him. But through it all, I had evidence that I was making disciplinary progress with the notorious group. When I first showed up at this school and indicated to them that I would demand a certain behavior, I found tender little notes on some desktops such as f— you K— By the end of the year, the phrases had become f— you *Mr.* K—. I had made a difference in the big suburban school, or so I thought.

Close to the end of the school year, one of the students in the lower tier, a very nice, responsible, sophomore girl told me that I should teach in college. She said that I was too smart and too good to be teaching the kids in high school, especially classes like the lower tier. She was well aware of being assigned to a lower tier class. I responded that she and her classmates in a lower tier class were just as important as any other students at any level. Then I thanked her for her thoughts and told her that I was making a move that could indeed lead to college teaching. The student in the lower tier class was interested in my future and giving me advice.

During this last year of teaching high school science, I had many serious thoughts about my future in the world of education. My ambitions included a Ph.D. in a scientific field, preferable genetics and cell biology. I wanted to teach in a rather small college, preferably a private college. Living in a relatively small city with a population of 25,000 to 40,000 would be ideal. And obviously it would be a college town with one or more colleges, which would be still another plus. College towns tend to be vibrant places with all the youth and a plethora of athletics events, theater, visiting scholars and speakers, music, and other performances. All these objectives were on my wish list, and I was hell bent on embarking on the journey to make them a reality, regardless of a few minor obstacles like having a family with five young children and possessing very little money.

On my way home following my last day of teaching in high school, I kept thinking about things like no more lesson plans; no more hall duty; no more wearing suits, sport coats, and ties. Some of us had always hypothesized that wearing ties by men was the main factor of why women lived longer than men. A tie puts an awful amount of pressure on those large blood vessels in the neck. However, a severe case of sadness crept in as I dodged in and out of the Twin Cities rush hour traffic. I had taught at the high school level for fourteen years—on the Iron Range, in an agricultural part of the state, and at a Saint Paul suburban school. My anticipated move was not due to burn out. The move was simply due to seeking a change. And I thought that even if I became a very effective researcher, I would still insist on teaching, unlike many others with advanced degrees. I needed to teach.

Chapter 11
Going for Broke—Literally

I was the first one on my mother's side of the family to obtain any kind of college degree, let alone graduate degrees. Not everyone in the family network understood graduate school education and the quest for higher degrees. Several years of working on master's degrees and then going back to school again for a Ph.D. prompted a few family members to surmise how dumb I must be to have to continually go back to school.

Beginning a Ph.D. program was a bit frightening, however, because I had a wife and five young children. I knew that I would be competing with a lot of bright young minds. But I always thrived on competition in the past, both in and out of school, so why not have another go-around. I began working for a noted cytogeneticist, Charles Burnham, who had a widespread reputation at the university for being tough. When I first met with him, he pulled out my file and studied my records for a few minutes. My GRE scores were much higher in the quantitative parts than the written comprehensive parts. He told me that if I needed to talk at any time, I should do so with numbers, and not with words. In the first week, when other graduate students asked me who I was working with, I would tell them, and they would simply say, "Sorry." A week or two later, I learned that Professor Burnham, who also served as my advising professor, flunked one of his students in the final written examination for the doctorate degree. My reaction was one of astonishment and more than a little alarm. As it turned out, Charlie Burnham and I got along very well. Contrary to popular belief, he was not intolerable. He just liked hard work and wanted his advisees to know their stuff. Although we had a couple of disagreements along the way, Professor Burnham turned out to be a good guy and a valued friend.

My organic chemistry background was a little dated, and it was mutually decided that I should take another class or two on the subject. Consequently, I found myself in a class of 260 students. I had my hand up to ask a question during most of the course and never got acknowledged by the professor once. This initial class was a big school baptism. One time, I went to the professor's office to discuss some kind of biochemical conformation. The line outside his office was like the ticket office for a World Series game. I hated lines so I said the heck with it, and I tried to figure it out on my own.

One should realize that most organic chemists are all from the same mold. They write with one hand and erase what they wrote with the other hand as they transverse the board from one end to the other like a robot. There must be a gene for such actions. I recall the story about a diligent student trying to keep up and write everything on the board into his notebook. But finally he had to give up. The student threw down his pencil and screamed out, "How am I supposed to keep up with this dash across the board?" The professor retorted, "That's your problem," and just kept going. Stories like that would always make me think about whether I should really be there. Sometimes I wondered if they would like me to show them how to drink a glass of water while standing on my head.

Most of the time I was quite impressed with my professors. I thought that they were some of the best teachers I ever had. And they didn't wear suits and ties. Some of them wore jeans—my kind of people. None of them ever had an education course in their entire life. They were Ph.D. individuals trained to be researchers but thrown into the classroom to teach. Of course, they were teaching subjects in which they were experts and biological topics that I liked. I actually planned on adopting some of their techniques when I got back into the classroom.

I did manage, however, to tick off one of the professors. He was a visiting professor from the University of California who was teaching a course in plant morphology. His labs were long and tedious because he was all about old-school methods, and he made us carefully diagram everything we observed in the microscope. My reaction was that this procedure was terribly old-fashioned. So one day I came into the laboratory with a microscope adapter and my camera. I shot photomicrographs of the tissues we were studying that day within minutes and then left much earlier than everyone else. The professor was between angry and livid. His thinking was that you tend to learn the material much better when you took the time to meticulously diagram it. When the first exam approached, I wrote a perfect exam, but the irate professor knocked off four points (still an A) for something superfluous. He admitted that the four-point reduction was on purpose because my camera antics pissed him off. We *compromised*, and I diagrammed everything his way during the remainder of the course. And thereafter we got along fine.

As it turned out, graduate school academics were the least of my problems. Having a ton of biological experience, via education and teaching, more than neutralized the age difference between me and the "bright young minds." However, how can someone do total residency in graduate school with a wife and five children? It was necessary to do studying very late at night. Also we were a family with a wife who as a mother wisely didn't want to find employment until all of the children were in school. Therefore, those three arduous years required a lot of financial craftiness for sheer survival. We had sold our previous house on a contract for deed. We cashed in all of my Minnesota teacher retirement. I had a couple of small scholarship awards, a graduate school assistantship, and some student loans. I also continued doing some freelance photography. I developed several sets of botanical and genetic 35 mm transparencies that I marketed to high schools and colleges. The venture was not a financial windfall, but it did help our anemic budget.

We turned to credit unions and their ridiculously high interest loans when necessary. Nonetheless, I was thankful that these loan companies had enough faith in us to repay the loans. I had to be a terrible risk. In severe emergencies, we resorted to something that is probably illegal. We had checking accounts at two banks in different suburbs. I would cash a check at some business establishment to get cash. The next day, I would cash an even larger check someplace on the other bank account. This cash allowed me to make a deposit into the previous bank account to cover the previous check with some cash left over. This game of raising the ante each day would continue until both accounts could be covered with some real money. I hope that the statute of limitations has expired.

The other side of being paupers was to find ways to save money in our daily lives. So we had a big garden. And we made our own wine out of beets. This wine was absolutely God-awful. Besides, we were stupid by making it in a large aluminum container. I should have taken even more organic chemistry. My wife, Rose, couldn't drink it, but I did. Most of the time it was the only affordable ethanol in the house.

At the University of Minnesota, I saved a little money by elimi-nating parking fees when possible. I was studying and researching plant genetics, and around those buildings on the campus there were always a lot of trucks, service vehicles, and other field equipment. I had an old Chevy carryall van, and I kept some empty wooden boxes in the back of the carryall. Then on frequent occasions I would simply back up to a yellow painted curb, open the rear door, and place the boxes so as to appear like things were being loaded or unloaded. This caper worked almost to perfection until I eventually did get a ticket at the main library on the Minneapolis campus. The other ploy was to give sweet corn from the plant genetics research fields to several meter maids. All they had to do was to put my Chevy carryall into their memory bank. I'm not sure whether this bit of graft worked or if I was just lucky.

Student loans were also available if you qualified for them. To obtain a student loan, you had to thoroughly fill out forms estimating all of your expenses and available income. Carefully following all of the guidelines, I did manage to get a student loan. A few days later, I also received a small scholarship. A few days after that, my student loan was reduced by the amount of the scholarship. A few days after that, I was in the office of a financial official emphatically complaining. He explained to me how all of the income from all of the sources made up a package of a certain size. So I took the lead and summarized what he told me. Income can change, right? He said absolutely. Well then, I continued, if income can change so can expenses. I went through the list of expenses and increased many of the items a little until the total of the increases equaled the size of my scholarship. I shoved the application back to him, and he stared at it for a moment. Then he called me an S.O.B. and stamped an approval on it. I won! On the way home, I bought a six-pack of real beer. The homemade beet wine was becoming unbearable.

Graduate school was not completely grueling work. Our genetics graduate school basketball team in the intramural league was pretty darn good. As I recall, four of us had previously played varsity basketball in college. Our team was called the "phages." No one knew what the heck a phage was all about. A phage is a virus that attacks bacteria, an often-studied system in genetics. Our team was quite a machine, winning the graduate school intramural championship and getting runners up in the overall university intramural program. All my life

I had wanted to play in the famous and historical Williams Arena at the University of Minnesota, fondly called, the "Big Barn." Finally at a not so young age on an intramural team, I had made it (the intramural championship game)—a dream that actually came true.

One fellow on our team was a gangly 6'4" individual and an excellent forward. He was from Tennessee, and while in Minnesota, he decided that he should learn how to ice skate and act like a Minnesota native. At the outdoor ice rink, he was a complete disaster. Arms and legs went in all directions before gravity would ultimately send him into a 6'4" prostrate position. He crawled to the outer wood fence and was hugging it when another guy came by and flopped perfectly on his butt. Our friend from Tennessee said to the fallen skater, "You must be from Tennessee." The guy got up brushing himself off and said "Yes, how did you know?"

The genetics graduate students also had a very good slow-pitch softball team in the men's intramural league. Partway through the schedule, a female postdoctorate researcher in molecular biology decided that she should be able to play. Being reasonable people, we let her play right field. Most of the opponents batted right-handed and would, therefore, hit the ball to left field. But then during the first game, there was this loud whining coming from right field. The sense of these outcries was, Why couldn't a woman pitch? Why does a man always get to pitch? So we let our token new player pitch. She had an awful time getting the ball across the plate. I was playing shortstop and spent a lot of time playing cat and mouse in the infield ground with the second baseman.

A few years later, she left science, became a state legislator, and was instrumental in getting the no smoking in restaurants law (except in designated areas) passed for Minnesota, the first in the country. She was a very strong-willed woman, and if anyone could ram that controversial bill through the legislature in spite of a strong opposing lobby, it would be her. Being allergic to cigarette smoke, my feelings toward our female right fielder/pseudo-pitcher changed favorably since our softball days.

I found that most of the graduate students who I interacted with were interesting people, but there were always a few with an attitudinal problem. Almost all of the Chinese students were easy-going cooperative people, except for this one Chinese fellow in our laboratory who thought that he pooped ice cream. He continually bitched about everything. Finally, I couldn't take it anymore, and in my usual tactful way I told him that if he didn't like it here, he should ship his skinny butt back to China. The next day he was gone. My advisor, who was also the Chinese guy's advisor, expressed to me that he didn't know what had happened. The Chinese graduate student left the university, presumably back to China, without any explanation. I acted surprised and responded that I had no idea why he decided to leave.

Something that I enjoyed very much was meeting many famous visiting scientists, some of them Nobel Prize awardees. This poor kid who used to scrape coal off the railroad tracks and grain from around the elevators in a small farming community was actually meeting and talking with Nobel Prize winners. Most notable among them was the mysterious and brilliant Barbara McClintock. She received the Nobel Prize for amassing evidence that genes did not always remain in one place in chromosomes; rather, they could jump around from one place to another. She was a very intense person and scared the heck out of me when I tried to explain my research project to her.

George Beadle, another Nobel Prize winner, was a very nice man. I had a super conversation with him at a cocktail party. He accidentally spilled his cocktail on me. I didn't even want to wash those pants. Professor Beadle had discovered what genes actually do on a molecular level.

My encounter with Adrian Srb was an interesting one. At that time, Professor Srb (Cornell University) was the sole author of the number-one college genetics textbook in the country. At lunch, I asked him what was really new on the genetics scene. He offered an explanation of recent research by investigators showing that caffeine impedes the DNA repair mechanisms in our cells. Professor Srb continued the discussion by pointing out that he personally would not drink coffee previous to having x-rays (radiation can break chromosomes). Throughout this discussion, the eating of his salad, his main entry, and dessert, he smoked cigarettes almost nonstop. He was a chain smoker and yet worried about the combination of a cup of coffee and an x-ray.

During the first year of graduate school, I was assigned to be a research assistant, and I really missed teaching. Research was fun, but I longed to get back into the classroom. So when one of my professors would ask me to substitute for him or her, I jumped at the opportunity. One evening, a professor called and asked me to teach his undergraduate genetics course for him the next day because he had to go out of town. The subject was the genetic code. I thought that I did a good job explaining the concept and its significance to the class (about seventy of them). Following the lecture, a rather plump male student sprawled out in his chair in the front row sarcastically asked, "What does any of this have to do with life?" Jeez, my lower tier junior high students wouldn't ask a dumb question like that. Of course, I lost my composure a little; in fact, I went a little ballistic. The entire discussion was about the basis of life. If he wasn't so darn big, I would have grabbed him by the back of his collar and the seat of his pants and ushered the crabby one out of the building. I was never asked to substitute for this class again. Over the next two years, I was a teaching assistant and back in my realm. Throughout my three full-time years at the university, I took as many pertinent classes as time permitted. I thought that a versatile biological background would better lead me to a position in a small college, where versatility was usually necessary.

Earning a Ph.D. requires an intense research project because a Ph.D. is essentially a research degree. Hence, a graduate student and his or her advisor must set research objectives, and these objectives have to be met. If not, you can expect to be around your university much longer than expected while you attempt to bring the research to some other fruition. I had a wife, five children, debts, and barely enough financial resources to somehow survive three years. Therefore, any lengthening of this quest for the degree was an option that scared the daylights out of me. Adding to my concern was the unpredictability of plant genetics research that I was conducting with maize (corn). I needed three good summer growing seasons to meet the outlined genetic objectives of the project. So what was there to worry about? Gophers go down the row digging up kernels and eating your research. Deer and coon invade your research field to eat your research. A reckless driver playing NASCAR smashes through the fence and plows into your field. Vandals pull out all of your stakes that marked the different cultures. Violent storms render your corn plants horizontal with the ground. A tornado flattens a house across the street from my research field. Somehow my research survived all of these catastrophes.

The completion of the research project only left the final oral examination for the Ph.D. degree; however, there was a rather long waiting period involved. I read in the university catalogue that this waiting period could be shortened by petition. I wanted to hurry through the final requirements so that I could advertise myself as a Ph.D. for academic positions. I found out that no one in the big university knew how to accelerate the process by petition. I was sent from office to office to office. As a last resort, I walked into the vice president's office and demanded to see him. The startled receptionist at the desk said that a person couldn't just walk in to see the vice president of the university. I countered with much determination that I was not leaving until I saw him. Certainly a big wheel like that would know how to handle my simple request. The receptionist immediately got on the phone and arranged everything regarding my petition within five minutes. Actually I fully intended to go to the president of the university next. I never got to see the big guy in the next room.

My advisors at the university were great. Charles Burnham was a master of cytogenetic concepts (chromosomes and cell division). His famous comment about the intricacies of chromosome behavior was that "Everything was intuitively obvious." Maybe everything was intuitively obvious to Professor Burnham, but not to everyone else. Ronald L. Phillips (coadvisor) impressed me as a super thinker. He could see important ramifications in what microscopic observations were showing and what experimental data were revealing better than anyone I have known. It was a privilege to work with these two superb scientists. Both advisors, and especially Professor Burnham, wanted me to concentrate on research. They maintained that I was someone of big university caliber. But I wanted a position that required ample teaching. Professor Burnham eventually accepted my strong desire to teach and became receptive to my plans. I just had to teach.

As my final oral exam approached, I was certain that I had a growth in my throat. I went to the university doctor who couldn't find any problem in that particular anatomy. He said, you must have finals coming up, and you are experiencing a nervous spasm in your throat. I felt that I was too cool a person for such a weakness, so I went to a throat specialist in Minneapolis who couldn't find any problem either. He said, you must have finals coming up, and you are experiencing a nervous spasm in your throat. Sure enough, after passing the final exam, the problem disappeared and never returned.

I now had a Ph.D. and a license to be eccentric, maybe even weird like some of the others who had earned the degree. My stepfather, a very good carpenter, asked, "What do you actually do anyway?" Explaining your scientific work to your parents is not an easy task. I thought we should begin the conversation gently with some basics. I asked him whether he knew what a chromosome was all about. He answered, "Of course I do. A chromosome is like a germ." I thought that we should probably forget about what I do. It wasn't important.

A famous photograph in the history of genetics. From left to right: Charles Burnham and Marcus Rhoades, both of whom were leading plant cytogenticists in the country. In the center is R. A. Emerson who was the mentor of these talented geneticists. Barbara McClintock (far right) and George Beadle (in the front) both won the coveted Nobel Prize for their work. Charles Burnham was my Ph.D. advisor. Note the tassel and ear bags, used to make controlled crosses with maize, stuffed into their belts. The photograph was taken when they were all researching at Cornell University in Ithaca, New York.

Charles Burnham was my advisor while attending graduate school at the
University of Minnesota. Professor Burnham was one of the leading plant
cytogeneticists in the country. *(Courtesy of R. L. Phillips)*

While attending graduate school at the University of Minnesota, I was able
to meet and talk with many famous scientists. Barbara McClintock won the
Nobel Prize for her research that showed the movement of certain genes
among chromosomes, now called transposable elements.

Ronald L. Phillips was a coadvisor to me.
Professor Phillips was a premier molecular cytogeneticist and an exceptional scholar. He was instrumental in my research endeavors. Professor Phillips is an elected member of the prestigious National Academy of Science.
(Courtesy of the University of Minnesota, David L. Hansen)

George Beadle also won the Nobel Prize. His most famous research was the determination of exactly what genes do. This work, called one gene-one enzyme, helped to set the stage for the subsequent burst of activity in molecular genetics. I found Beadle to be a really nice, down-to-earth guy.

(Courtesy of George Beadle, Special Collections, Oregon State University)

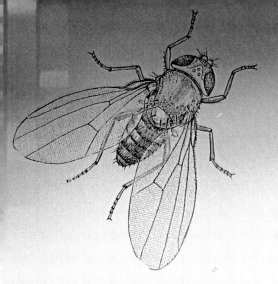

Part III
FINALLY BECOMING
A PROFESSOR

Chapter 12
Teaching in College

The Ph.D. degree was finalized too late for conducting an adequate job search for the upcoming academic year, that is, for a tenured-track position. The next best situation was to find a temporary one-year position. College professors get awarded sabbaticals, suffer illnesses, and take leaves of absence for various reasons like grants, fellowships, or even a need to dry out. One of those temporary one-year positions was a possible opportunity to teach at my undergraduate alma mater, Winona State University. The position called for a person with expertise in genetics and plant morphology. The job description for this background was not the most common combination, but I was a perfect fit. Also it was only a temporary position, which would greatly limit the number of applicants. Besides all of that, I was an alumnus, supposedly an added bonus. It wasn't so long ago when I thought that I was a popular guy on campus. With much confidence, I told my wife that she could begin packing for the move to Winona.

Lo and behold, I did not get the job. I didn't even get a rejection letter. Not long after this personal setback while living in Winona and working at the other four-year college in the city, by happenstance I ran into a number of professors in the Winona State University Biology Department. All of them were quick to tell me that they wanted me for that position. Interestingly, the math didn't add up.

Fortunately, I connected on one of those temporary one-year appointments at the University of Wisconsin, River Falls, not far from the Twin Cities where we were still living. This bit of luck did not require a family move, and it allowed me an entire year to seek a tenured-track position. I was absolutely elated to be back in the classroom, and now I had so much to teach them. One thing that I could not teach the nice people from across the border was that other professional football teams had the right to exist besides the Green Bay Packers. This situation was not a serious matter, but a Minnesota guy, worse yet a Vikings fan, had come into their space. Most of the difference in allegiance was good-natured fun, that is, most of the time. The tension between the two states reminded me of the Wisconsin poet with a home on the bank of the St. Croix River directly across from Minnesota. When asked by a reporter during an interview why he had a cannon in his yard pointed at Minnesota, he responded, "That just because they haven't attacked yet, doesn't mean they are not going to eventually do so."

Anti–Vietnam War activities were rampaging, and every once in a while I would find out that a former student was killed in action. Such news was hard to take. This period of turmoil was not a fun time.

During this first year of my college teaching career at River Falls, my advisor and mentor at the University of Minnesota decided to retire, and I was asked to give a talk at his retirement banquet being held in the Coffman Memorial Hall on the university campus. I was his very last graduate student. I wondered whether I drove him into it. After my classes at River Falls, I intended to hurry home and put on a suit and tie (the only one such outfit I had) for the gala event. Geneticists rarely wear suits and ties; however, because of the retiree's distinction and fame, this was a special occasion. But the college students at the university where I was teaching had blocked all of the highways in and out of the city. The blockade was another anti-war demonstration. So I went to a service station to get some information as to how I might get out of town. Down a couple of alleys I went, over a narrow dirt road, through a dumping ground, and onto the highway outside of town. I had made it.

Next I drove to the University of Minnesota all dressed up for my big talk. Arriving in the proximity of Coffman Memorial Hall, a nice police officer informed me that I couldn't get there because of an anti-war demonstration blocking Washington Avenue. Spelling out my predicament prompted the officer to get me to Coffman Memorial Hall by a roundabout way on River Road. A huge crowd was present for the ceremony so I guess they all got there by the roundabout way too or they all owned helicopters. I couldn't believe it. I was turned back by two barricading incidents in one day. Again, it was not a fun period of time.

On an upside of things, I could tell that teaching in college was going to be an interesting and enjoyable experience. Freshly coming out of graduate school made me feel that I knew absolutely everything, and I expected my students to learn absolutely everything. In the beginning, my grading might have been a little harsh. I had a lot of student visits to my office. Men usually complained and women usually cried. I spent my own money on tissues. But I began to think that maybe I really did expect too much.

Some of the gnashing of teeth regarding grades, and even a few failing grades, was not entirely my fault. The university was in the midst of conducting a large educational program to induce young people from indigent families to attend college and hopefully do well. Most of the students in this group simply didn't try, no matter how hard I (and other teachers) tried to get them to try. College counselors were well aware of the situation and also made very little progress in changing their attitudes. Sometimes absolutely nothing works, and it is downright frustrating. And sadly this situation was taking place at a good university.

Toward the end of the year while at River Falls, I was once again faced with the throes of job hunting. The professor I replaced had been on a sabbatical leave, and against my hopes, he decided to return. Therefore, I was out of work and jobs were still relatively scarce, which once again created a great amount of anxiety. I was offered a post-doctorate position at Southern Illinois University that I declined. I wanted to forsake postdoctorate work and get right into a tenured-track position. I was offered a position at Clemson University as a U.S. Department of Agriculture (USDA) scientist but it was all research, and I wanted to teach. I was an applicant finalist at the University of Idaho, which was beautiful country but a low pay scale; hence, I withdrew my application. Finally, I managed to find a tenured-track teaching job at Saint Mary's University of Minnesota, a small private liberal arts college in Winona located in the beautiful southeastern part of the state. Because of attending the "other college" in Winona for my undergraduate degree and a master's of education degree, I knew the Winona area well and was elated to return. During my interview with the search committee, I indicated to the search committee that I could teach just about anything—maybe even wash dishes in the cafeteria. I badly wanted that job.

When I related my good news of being offered the Saint Mary's University job to the department chairperson at the Wisconsin school, he said that I would probably like it better at the other college. But I really liked it at the present college. It was a one-year position and I had to leave. The chairperson almost seemed happy that I was leaving. Some of the prized straight "A" students had received "C" grades in my genetics course. At any rate, I was still in the workforce.

Every time I began work in a new school, I was given a faculty handbook. A faculty handbook is kind of a bible for the school. I was supposed to read it in order to know how the place was governed, what I could and could not do, what rights I had, and so forth. I had jumped from the high school in southern Minnesota, to the Twin Cities suburban high school, to the University of Minnesota, to the public university in River Falls, Wisconsin, to the private college in Winona, Minnesota, all within a seven-year span. The result of this nomadic life was five faculty handbooks in seven years, and I had never read much of any of them. I pretty much guessed about doing things on the job.

The first week at the new position in Winona brought some interesting interactions with my new colleagues. One of the first persons I met at a reception welcomed me to the college and said that he hoped I would enjoy my stay and that it would be a long successful partnership. In my mind, I was thinking this job was going to be a stepping stone. I took the job because of my familiarity with Winona, and it paid more than the University of Idaho. However, another big plus was that the college had an excellent reputation in biological education. Although I was elated about having the position, I was still thinking that I would be on my way to bigger places within a few years. I have often thought about that stepping-stone plan over the following forty years during which time I never had any urge to leave, in spite of having several opportunities.

One of my first lunches in the faculty dining room didn't go very well. A faculty member who taught in the language department somehow learned that my real name was changed from the Polish version to a shorter version. This colleague was originally from the Polish/Ukraine region, and he proceeded to give me a lecture for changing my name. I had never changed the name because my parents legally made the name change when I was born. Nonetheless, I didn't think that I owed him an explanation. The comment that I defiantly shot back relayed that I didn't think I had to defend my name to people who I assumed to be intelligent and educated. He left me alone after that.

Another lunch soon after didn't go well either. One of the faculty philosophers greeted me less than enthusiastically. I immediately could tell that he was anti-science. Geneticists run into these people all of the time. College politics generated by your field of study is ubiquitous. He asked me whether I had read some philosophical book with a better-than-thou look on his face. I said no, and then asked him whether he had read the *Double Helix* by James Watson. He said no and then asked me whether I had read some other book. I said no and then asked him whether he had read *The Origin of Species* by Charles Darwin. He said no and then asked me whether I had read another book. I said no and then asked him whether he had read *The Selfish Gene* by Richard Dawkins or *Silent Spring* by Rachel Carson. Neither of us had crossed the academic line. It was obvious that both of us were illiterate in each other's field, but at least I didn't sneer during the book match like he did.

My early encounters with students also proved to be quite interesting. These students were not only hard working, but also proud of their academic work ethic. When I met with a class for the very first time, I always had a habit of simply introducing myself and then immediately embarking into a substantial lecture. I was never keen about dilly-dallying around with boring introductory garbage concerning class protocol. At some places, this technique would catch the class off guard, but these biology majors were prepared for action with pen, notebook, and the right attitude. Many of them were hell-bent on becoming M.D.s. Serious students yes, but I still sensed that they wanted their teachers to be more to them than someone plastering the board with biological information. It was almost like we were family and that bonding was important to many of them—at least a togetherness sort of bonding without striving to be teacher's pets.

Early during the first term, I returned an exam in my cell biology course. These students were mostly juniors and biology majors, well screened already and accustomed to good and even excellent grades. Several of the students chose to argue a particular point on the exam, but it was obvious to me that their answer to the question was wrong. I was congenial about the disagreement; however, I had to hold my ground because they were indeed wrong, and that fact couldn't be ignored. When I found the issue becoming tiresome, which didn't take too long, I asserted with some finality that their answer was wrong, that they would not get credit for it, and that if they didn't like it—after a short hesitation—they could burn a cross on my front lawn. We then moved on to another topic. Then, on a drizzling Halloween evening, my wife and I could hear strange-sounding chants outdoors. Upon investigating the situation, four or five persons in dark hoods were trying to light a wooden cross in our front lawn. They couldn't get it lit because of the heavy drizzle, and when I approached the crime scene I pointed out to them that they must be from the cell biology class because they couldn't do anything right. They laughed, removed their hoods, and came in the house, and we all raided the refrigerator. I have always hesitated to tell this story because of its racial implications. I don't think that such a thought ever entered the students' minds.

When Halloween came around the next year, several of the students (now seniors) mentioned that they might stop in to see us again. I emphatically pointed out that there should be no burning of crosses. However, they liked to be in the company of some of their teachers and more importantly the contents of their teacher's refrigerator. I warned my wife that some of the individuals knocking on our door that evening would be big kids from the college, and that she shouldn't give them candy. They want more substantial food and drink. Indeed several of them did show up, and we congregated in the kitchen where we engaged in conversation. My wife went to answer the next knock on the front door where she found a rather tall individual in a mask and costume holding out a bag for treats. Because of his size, she thought he must be another college guy and told him to come in. He hesitated so she grabbed him by the arm and tried to lead him into the house. The costumed person in a weak and very concerned voice said, "Look lady, all I want is candy." The tall youngster thought he was going to get the tricks rather than the treats.

I found teaching in college to be just as much fun as it was in high school. It was evident that I would still have ample opportunities to goof around. And without any doubt, I was acutely aware that there would be important decisions to make, problems to resolve, responsibilities, and difficulties. The beginning years are the hardest, and one must be prepared to work long hours, sometimes as much as sixty to seventy hours per week; not because you are a workaholic, but because getting the job done right required that much time. Late nights at the desk in my home were frequent events, especially due to an attempt to keep up with the scientific literature that changed constantly. Weekends were often filled with getting caught up.

The transition from high school to college teaching brought on a raft of decisions. What textbooks should I use? How much depth is appropriate at this level of education? What kind of grading procedure should I use? What kind of pedagogy might work best? How friendly should I be with the students? I would like to be friends with the students, but more importantly, I wanted to be their teacher, that is, their mentor. Some salvation to all of this decision making has been called teacher's academic freedom.

I was looking forward to teaching very bright students, but even in college the classes tended to be somewhat heterogeneous with regard to academic ability. Some of the students impressed me as being bright enough to get straight "A" grades no matter where they chose to go to college. Then there were some students who maybe shouldn't have gone to college. One of the favorite stories I heard involved one of the professors in a different department. It went something like the following. A visitor was looking into various classrooms to get a feel for what was going on. He approached one classroom in which the door was open, and the students appeared to be working on an assigned task at their desks. In a soft tone so as not to cause an interruption, the visitor asked the professor what he was teaching today. Without any hesitation, the professor blurted out in a loud voice, "Idiots." Days like that do happen, even with college students. However, for me most days had enough fun and excitement in them whereby I always enjoyed going back the next day.

I must, however, relate a real example of why some teachers lose their hair sooner than normal, even while teaching the "bright" college students. A colleague of mine came stumbling out of her introductory biology lab almost with tears in her eyes. She was teaching them basic microbiological techniques in which you should always flame the inoculating needle in a Bunsen burner before dipping it into the bacterial culture. In the next exercise designed to show them the ever presence of bacteria, the students were to set up some agar plates in various ways. For example, they were to touch a coin to the agar in one case, swab the doorknob and touch the swab to the agar in another case, and touch the agar with one of their fingers in still another case. One of the students flamed her finger in the burner before touching the agar. I reiterate that this episode took place in college, and one has to wonder about that student's ACT score.

In the field of science, laboratory sessions are usually taught in conjunction with the classroom activities. It is in these smelly laboratories where a lot of odd things can happen, some of which make you angry, some of which make you laugh, and some of which almost make you cry. I cannot even guess how many items of clothing I have ruined in these labs by leaning on the surfaces of lab tables left with remnant chemical spills and stains. Elbow regions in shirts and sweaters can completely disappear in a few days. One female student spilled an entire flask of sodium azide on herself. She had to be the recipient of an immediate shower, clothes and all. Now that was an interesting day.

Most laboratory goofs occurred spontaneously, but I must confess that I caused a few of these episodes. Students doing electrophoresis for the first time was great fun. Electrophoresis is a technique whereby you separate different molecules with an electric current in a gel-like substance, at that time, within glass tubes. Of course there are positive and negative ends that should be hooked up correctly, and I gave the students the wrong information. Reversing the connections caused the noodle-like gels to pop out of the tubes into the air-like Asian carp leaping out of water.

Then there was the female student with long straight hair down to her waist trying to read the numbers on a Gilson respirometer. This instrument is a large sophisticated water bath with tiny emerged flasks being shaken back and forth. As she got close to the digital apparatus to record a reading, her long hair got into the water bath and tangled up into the shaking apparatus. Therefore, her long hair went back and forth, back and forth in the water bath without her knowing it for some time. We all just watched in amazement as the hair went back and forth, but we should have added some shampoo. And I got paid for doing this stuff.

Things were not always funny. One student placed a rotor into the high-speed centrifuge without it being properly seated and secured on the axle. These rotors are made of titanium, and they are extremely heavy. They are also very expensive. When a rotor accidentally comes off of the central axle at an extremely high speed, it results in an excruciating sound, much worse than a bowling ball in a rolling clothes dryer. Of course, this mishap ruined the rotor (about $5,000) and the drum of the machine (about another $5,000). Today, it would be more like a $20,000 to $30,000 mistake.

I admit that sometimes I was a devilish troublemaker. Once I came into a lab session consisting of nonscience majors with a stool that was nothing more than a toilet seat on kind of a folding lawn chair. With a straight face, I pointed out that we were going to do some urine analyses. We needed a volunteer to provide some pee. Who would like to be first? What is great about working with nonscience majors is that they are awe-struck in the science building and believe everything you tell them. On another occasion, we did a lab exercise in which each student microscopically checked his or her own inner cheek cells for Barr bodies. These microscopic bodies are tiny densely stained structures that one can observe in the cells with a good microscope. Females (if with normal chromosomes) have one Barr body per cell, actually a nucleus, and males (if with normal chromosomes) do not have any Barr bodies. Deviations from these observations would indicate that the individual probably has a sex chromosome abnormality. Nonscience students couldn't tell Barr bodies from fly poop on the slide in the microscope. So I could easily convince a female student that she had no Barr bodies or a male student that he did have Barr bodies. The victims of this warped sense of humor would almost run out of the lab crying before I could own up to my immature behavior. Some teachers should really grow up.

Nonscience majors were such easy targets because of their gullibility. One couldn't resist fooling around with them. Once in a while I would purposefully bait them in the midst of a discussion and then give them hell for not seeing through it. After admitting that I was only baiting them, I would add that I was a master baiter. Most of the nonscience students wouldn't get it. I really hated to waste a good joke.

One other time I was teaching a nonscience major course called Heredity and Society that dealt with a mesh between genetics and social issues. At the beginning of the class, I was standing by the open doorway previewing our discussion for the day. We were going to talk about mutations in humans. At that precise moment, a colleague in the department was coming down the hallway. It was early in the academic year, and he was a new biology faculty member; hence, I was sure that none of the nonscience majors had ever seen him. To help matters, he was very pubescent (bearded) with sort of a hunchback posture. Impulsively, I pointed out to the class that I had a human mutant from an institution for them to observe. I grabbed his arm as he was going by and led him into the classroom. He immediately picked up on the prank and improvised in a way that would put most actors to shame. He pranced, huffed, and snorted. I pointed out how deranged he was, and I warned the class not to laugh at him because he would easily get upset. So no one laughed and I swear some of the students began taking notes. I eventually led him back to the doorway, pushed him into the hallway, and told the imaginary attendants that they could take him back now. Gosh, how I loved this job.

I think that it was the same class on another occasion in which

I was showing 35 mm slides of human mutations and developmental problems. This incident took place when I was showing the slide of Cyclops, one eye in the middle of the forehead of a newborn. That is when a student sitting in the second row completely disappeared from view. She had fainted and oh so smoothly slid under the seat in front of her. Waving some air at her soon brought her back to consciousness. But the incident precipitated a rumor around campus that I had given her mouth-to-mouth resuscitation and kept it up for fifteen minutes after she had revived. Not true!

Another spontaneous incident with sexual innuendoes occurred when I asked a female student where she had placed a particular dissection tool that I needed. She told me that the tool was in a drawer at her workstation in the research lab down the hall. This student was doing a research project, and an area in that particular lab was set aside for students to work. As I walked down the hallway toward the research lab, the student yelled out loudly, "Keep your hands out of my drawers." Instantaneously, five or six heads popped out of various rooms and labs up and down the hallway.

Sometimes my antics had very unexpected outcomes. I was teaching some of the "bright" students in a course that was part of the honor's program at the university. The course was called Great Ideas in Science and Math, and I was team teaching it with a mathematics professor. We would, for the most part, alternate days when we would teach the group. On this one day, the mathematician demonstrated something about tomography. He showed that he could remove the vest he was wearing without removing his sport coat. The students loved it.

Neither the mathematician nor I ever admitted it, but throughout the course, we were in subtle competition with each other. So during the next period, I informed the students that I would take off my underwear without removing my pants. Well of course, I had simply stuffed some jockey shorts up my pant leg before coming to class. As I went into my contortions, I couldn't get the darn underwear to flop out. After a super great Elvis Presley impersonation, the underwear finally fell on the floor. Of course, the students loved the performance. After class, I answered a couple of questions, erased the board, picked up my teaching materials (including the underwear), and went down one flight of stairs. Within those few minutes of reaching the main floor, the president of the university approached me and said: "I hear you took your underwear off in class today." The president was a real Christian Brother, but was he an actual *big brother* with cameras in the classrooms? At any rate, the nut in the biology department appreciated the president's tolerance.

I stumbled into many other awkward situations. One of my classes was conducting an experiment that involved substances in test tubes. We have test tube racks for holding these tubes, but I noticed that all of the students were holding the tubes in their hands waiting for the next step—not good lab procedure, that is, all except one female student who had the test tubes stuffed into the front pocket of her blouse. I asked the class why they neglected to use a test tube rack, and then in an effort to be humorous I pointed out that this particular student had a nice rack. (I meant her pocket in the blouse.) The class burst into laughter. I immediately realized why. She indeed had a very nice "rack." Every day had its lighter moments.

The fun of teaching at this college just never ended. Although I never actively looked for another position, several opportunities came up, but I always resisted the move. However, I did interview for another position once. I never applied for the job, but they called me. The position was for a plant geneticist at a very large corporation that produced vegetables. I didn't want the job, but I interviewed for it anyway just to become more acquainted with the plant genetics that took place at the company. Consequently, I gave a poor interview. In fact, at times I was probably a big ass. Then they told me the starting salary, and I nearly fainted. Alas, it was too late because I had made my nest. Although I was a top three finalist, I didn't get the job. But seriously I didn't care because of a number of factors, not the least of which was the strong desire to stay involved in teaching.

Most of the Saint Mary's University of Minnesota campus located in the
lower hills above Winona, Minnesota. The University is a Catholic liberal
arts institution. *(Courtesy of Saint Mary's University)*

The Adducci Science complex consists of Hoffman and Severin Halls. I
spent forty wonderful years teaching and researching in the bowels of these
buildings. *(Courtesy of Saint Mary's University of Minnesota)*

During my teaching career, I had the privilege to meet many notable
and interesting people. Linus Pauling received the Nobel Prize for peace
and a second Nobel Prize for chemistry. I was able to talk with him for a
considerable amount of time before he gave a presentation in Winona.
(Courtesy of Linus Pauling, Special Collections, Oregon State University)

I was in the front row for a talk in Chicago by James D. Watson and was able to sneak in a greeting to the famous scientist. Watson won the Nobel Prize for his elucidation of the structure of the DNA molecule with Francis Crick. The encounter was an enjoyable event.

(Courtesy of National Human Genome Research)

Chapter 13

Chairing the Department— Not All Fun

A renewal contract was offered to me after the first year at my new position. At first I didn't notice, but soon after its contents hit me like an eighteen-wheel truck. In addition to my teaching duties, the contract stated that I was to be the chairperson of the biology department. The assignment was completely unexpected. The "real" administrators never even discussed this "pseudo-administrator" possibility with me. After racing to the office of the vice president for academic affairs and rushing through the closed door without opening it, I demanded an explanation. I was informed that the university had the right to assign these other duties as they saw fit. Of course the university gave me a little release time to handle the chores and a small stipend. I really mean a *little release time* and a *small stipend*. In a small university, you still keep a good proportion of your teaching load in addition to chairing the department. And as far as I could tell, the position was not at all prestigious; rather, it was just another assignment. I had always disliked administrators, not personally but because of the way they carried out their jobs and imposed themselves on everyone else. Now I was supposed to be one of them. In my opinion, many administrators sat around in big offices thinking of things that others should do. And unlike them, the others were too busy with teaching. And administrators always wanted the task done by tomorrow.

During that next academic year at the helm of the department, I was rather clueless. Heck, I didn't know the difference between a memo and a business letter. In addition, I didn't know how to write either one of them. Thankfully, we are given good secretaries. But now I had to deal with people on different terms. Some of my past experiences with people left a lot to be desired. Also, many of these academicians were not your average Joes. They tended to be bright, independent thinkers, but still in need of help on the job, especially in decision making. There were times when I thought my role was more like amateur psychiatrist than geneticist. Budgetary matters were easier for me to handle. I always overspent our family domestic budget, so I did the same as chairperson of the biology department. I soon adopted a philosophy: just do things the way I want to do them and beg for forgiveness later. That concept worked fairly well, some of the time. But I had to deal with a lot of people other than faculty, and it was not always a walk in the rose garden. For example, there were times when I had to interact with the heads of the cafeteria, finance office, business office, maintenance, bookstore, and presidential aids. I felt that these people were all cloned, with the same characteristic of wanting to give me (and everyone else) a hard time. It was my impression that these various heads all thought that they ran the college and that the teachers worked for them.

Interviewing applicants for openings in the department in a professional manner was both an important and difficult task. I never had any classes that covered how to go about interviewing people. I don't think that I ever became very good at this part of the job. I simply tried to learn how to do it while on the job. I vividly recall the first opening under my chairmanship. The search committee and myself sifted the applicants down to about five, and I called each of them in order to do a phone interview before deciding whom among them we would invite for a visit to our school. One of the applicants didn't know the geographic location of our university. I related my amazement to him that he wanted to be an environmental biologist at our university, took the time to apply, and didn't know where the heck the place was located nor its particular environment. He responded something like your city is "way up there, isn't it?" I replied, "Yes it is way up there, much farther way up there than you want to go." And then I hung up on him. Just like that we were down to four applicants. You can see, as a chairperson, I was steadily getting better at dealing with people.

After a few times, I was becoming a little better at handling interviews. The molecular biologist was in my office for the big interview, and he looked very uncomfortable. So I asked him if he would like to remove his sport coat. It came off in a nanosecond. We babbled a little more, and he still appeared uncomfortable. So I asked him if he would like to remove his tie. It came off in another nanosecond. I started to like the guy. He was completely frank about everything, and he really knew how to laugh. Next, we went out for drinks at cocktail hour; then drinks and dinner. Then we went to my home for after dinner drinks and more discussions. We both got pretty loose. The next day, I recommended that the university offer him the position. We hit it off, and I really needed a friend. He stayed with us for three years before moving on to positions in several large universities. We have been the best of friends ever since even though geographically separated for the past thirty years.

Recommending people to be hired can cause a person to sweat bullets, because you always wanted to hire someone you can work with on a daily basis, that is, someone who was a good fit. But recommending that someone not be renewed (also known as being fired) was even more difficult. As chairperson, I only did this dastardly deed once. Of course, I only pointed out that I would not recommend that his contract would be renewed. A faculty committee and the administration have the final say, mostly the latter. As he left my office, he slammed the door hard, and I heard the muttering of some nonprintable descriptive comments. That evening, my wife and I went to the Guthrie Theater in Minneapolis. I know that I was in attendance, but I really don't remember much about the production. About a year later, this person and I talked on the phone, and he was seemingly happy with his new job. The amicable conversation made me feel good.

For more than one reason, I was sure that not everyone danced around my chairmanship with glee. But at least there was always a never-fail way to reduce some of the tension, and that way was called ethanol. On some Friday afternoons after a particularly tough week embedded with rather abrasive encounters, I would purchase a quart of good Scotch whiskey, get a bucket of ice from our laboratory ice machine, and place a sign on the door that read MEETING IN PROGRESS, which of course was a lie. The biology staff would gather for an attitude adjustment, including those who didn't drink in bars or even at home. Without reading the faculty handbook, I was sure that this activity broke university rules. But again, I resorted to my motto, just do it and beg for forgiveness later.

Good Scotch didn't always guarantee cooperation from all of the staff members. Occasionally I did experience a falling out with a member of the department. After making out the class schedule for the next academic year, which was a very laborious task, a staff member in our department informed me that he wished to change his employment to part time rather than full time, and he had the administration's blessing. So I did the entire class schedule again, which was a very laborious task, in order to satisfy his wishes for part-time teaching. Then this individual complained about how I had arranged his part-time duties. By now, my fuse had become considerably shorter. So in a somewhat jesting-like way, I suggested that because he was so hard to satisfy, maybe he should just quit altogether. He didn't take it as jest, and he did quit altogether. I then made out the entire class schedule once again, which by the way, was a very laborious task.

I hated meetings with a passion. As a chairperson, there were so many of them such as department meetings, faculty meetings, chairperson meetings, and various committee meetings. When asked about what I did for a living, I often answered that I went to meetings. Faculty meetings were the worst kind. A large room would be full of Ph.D. and equivalent-degreed people all trying to display their intelligence, but never with any agreement. Following these meetings, I would often go home, climb the hill in my backyard, and stare into space. Pounding on an old concrete foundation behind my garage with a sledgehammer was also good therapeutic activity. But just like many of the meetings that I had to attend, the pounding on the concrete never accomplished anything.

Once I had to attend an evening meeting; however, our two cars were already in use due to activities by our sons and daughters. I didn't have enough time to walk, so I took the garden tractor, a big old Sears 16-hp machine. At night one can really see the combustion taking place in the engine lighting up like a giant firefly. I am sure that the neighbors thought I was crazy. But what the heck, such antics tend to keep the neighbors away.

Some faculty meetings could drive you insane. Once I pointed out that I didn't have any idea what the hell (exact words) I was voting on because of all the amendments to the amendments. I did a lot of abstaining. Several times rather than voting "yes" or "no" or "abstain," I added a category and voted "who cares." On another occasion, I asserted that the faculty could screw up a free lunch. Once when I was nominated for a particular committee in which I absolutely had no intention of being on, I responded to the nomination by saying that I would rather be poked in the eye with a sharp stick. I was asked whether this comment meant that I declined the nomination. How else could someone spell out declination? I would rather drink a pail full of warm spit?

Arguments with higher-up administrators seemed to be simply part of the job. One debate concerned how much teaching credit biology professors should get for teaching the laboratory part of their courses. Many of us involved in the teaching of labs actually did a lot of active teaching during that time period. We didn't just throw out some directions regarding the exercise and go have coffee. Consequently, I was arguing for the teaching credit to be increased, and the president of the university wanted things to remain as they were. Costs were usually the basis of most arguments. We exchanged memo after memo debating the situation. At one point as part of my argument, I sent him a memo asking how come this and how come that, and so forth. I received a response from him that stated things in a very simple way: "Because I am the president, and you are not." An abrupt end to the argument seemed appropriate, but we did eventually compromise.

Another function often relegated to a chairperson is to help woo potential benefactors. In one such case, an attempt was being made to entice a large foundation to increase its annual grant award to the biology department from five figures to six figures. An idea was hatched by the administration to wine and dine one of the chief guys of the foundation. The university arranged for an elaborate cocktail reception and a five-course dinner at one of the local mansions in the beautiful country hills, owned by a local well-to-do businessman. Of course, the biology chairperson and his spouse had to attend. I didn't mind too much because top drawer Scotch, gin, and other liquors were flowing freely.

It was at the shrimp cocktail course of the dinner where things went awry. The dinner guests were provided with gold forks (real gold forks) to devour jumbo shrimp. I loved shrimp and in my zeal to cut one of these large animals in half, I broke my gold fork into two pieces. But when I realized that no one had probably seen the mishap (not many of them were sober), I slyly placed the two pieces of the gold fork into my pocket with the intention of taking them to the kitchen later with a full explanation of what happened. After I got home and began to change into more comfortable clothes, I found the two pieces of the gold fork still in my pocket. The host would think that someone had stolen the gold fork. I returned the gold pieces to our gracious host by mail with an explanation and an offer to pay for its repair. I hoped he believed this unbelievable story. However, I was never invited back.

Safety was another issue that a department chairperson needed to constantly address. Separate storage rooms existed in our department under lock and key for toxins, flammables, carcinogens, drugs, and, yes, alcohol. While watching the news on television one evening, my attention was drawn to a picric acid problem. The substance was supposedly very explosive, and various schools were finding the dangerous stuff on their shelves in storage rooms. When the news report continued by showing bomb experts blowing up small quantities of picric acid in an open field, I thought that I had better check our stock rooms. The next day I found a rather large amount of the substance on a shelf in our chemical storeroom. I immediately notified university officials that we needed to get rid of this material. They were not keen on spending a lot of dollars to get a professional bomb squad to do the job, so they decided to handle the situation themselves. Their plan was to move the picric acid to a cave in the side of a steep hill on the edge of the campus that was secured by a heavy solid door and locks, at least as a temporary solution. I wanted no part of this scheme. So they asked me to at least clear the building, which I did. Then one of these courageous low-level administrator guys who didn't want to hire a bomb squad carried the picric acid carefully and slowly. The other courageous low-level administrator guy who didn't want to hire a bomb squad walked in front of him holding a sign that read: DANGER: EXPLOSIVES. They slowly made this death march all the way to the cave. This event should have been recorded.

Still another problem that occasionally ended up in the chairperson's office was vandalism. One time a very expensive Leitz research-grade microscope disappeared from one of our laboratories. A couple days later, I placed a short statement in the daily student publication of the university. The essence of this statement was that I knew who took the microscope, and should the microscope be returned to its place in the department, I wouldn't need to obtain a search warrant, and therefore, no charges would be filed. The next day, the microscope was back in its usual place. I never had any idea who took this microscope.

One time my office was also the scene of a crime. It was during mid-term break and very few faculty or students were around. I needed to go to the business office located in another building to handle a transaction. When I returned, a young man at the doorway of my building began asking me questions like where was the gymnasium. I suddenly became suspicious so I took a very discerning look at him. When I returned to my office, I thought that I had better check things out with more than a little scrutiny. Two expensive cameras were missing, and my checkbook had been lifted from my briefcase. Quickly running out and looking for the scoundrels was to no avail. The guy at the door was a very effective lookout.

When the police arrived, I described the guy at the door with a great amount of detail. I told them that the guy was about twenty years old, 5'10", about 165 pounds, dark short hair without a part, and a small U-shaped scar on the right side of his chin, and so forth. The police immediately knew who he was and where he lived. At about dinnertime that same evening, a clerk at a local convenience store called to ask whether I had written a check for $50 to a guy who was buying merchandise in his store. This guy and his girl companion were already in the process of leaving the parking lot in a car. I told the clerk to get his license number, which he did. That very same night about 2:00 a.m., the fourth (and last) of the merry bandits actually called me on the phone. He said the cops were waiting for him to come back to his apartment. Then he cried a little or pretended to do so. He wanted to know how expensive the cameras were and what he should do. I told him that the cameras were special and worth thousands of dollars (I lied) and that he should take the cameras to the police station and get the whole thing over with. Then I emphasized that he shouldn't call me at 2:00 a.m. ever again. The next day the detective on the case told me that the fourth suspect turned himself in around 2:30 a.m. I responded with an innocent "Really."

None of the wayward four were students at the university, and I agreed to press charges. Soon after, some guy came to my home claiming to represent the naughty ones and asked me to drop the charges. I almost physically removed him from my property. The bandits only got their hands slapped this time, but I saw in the local newspaper that the three males got into serious trouble a few months later. This time their antisocial behavior resulted in jail sentences. I understand that the girl accomplice straightened herself out. However, once again I became the subject of an ugly rumor on campus. Why always me? This time the story went as follows: I supposedly pressed charges against the three guys and made a deal with the girl. Again, absolutely not true!

In all probability, the chance to be chairperson opened up other opportunities like being a consultant for the biology department at the University of Wisconsin, River Falls. It was a relatively easy piece of work for the services that I rendered. It was money that my wife and I blew in one great weekend in the Twin Cities. Because of being the chairperson, I got to represent the university's science division at the Minnesota Board of Education in Saint Paul. Truthfully, I didn't understand a word that the education participants said. Upon leaving the meeting, I had two martinis and stared into space for a while.

Because I was chairperson, it was my job to handle a few parental complaints. Thank goodness there were very few irritated parents. One of my best interactions was when a parent complained that the department did very little to give his son, now a senior, direction for entering into an occupation. I pointed out that we had approximately twenty-five seminars each year times four years that his son was at the school, which totaled one hundred such seminars. These were seminars in which the speakers came from a wide variety of biological and medical occupations. And I never saw his son at any of them.

Regardless of a few downsides of being a pseudo-administrating chairperson, there was one very good advantage. I was in position to get things done. I started a weekly biology seminar series, a biology newsletter, an undergraduate biology research symposium for regional colleges and universities, and a speaker's bureau, and I was able to double the size of the biology teaching staff. With the help of others in the department, we added an environmental major and an allied health program. And I personally wrote grants that brought $1.1 million into the college coffers, much of which was used to purchase contemporary, sophisticated, biological instrumentation. So bitch as I may about being a part-time paper-pusher for seven long years, the job turned out to be worth all of the time consumption and occasional mayhem.

Chapter 14

Research and Never-Ending Grantmanship

Some of my college classmates who remained in K–12 teaching would often razz me about how little work college teachers did. Of course, they were referring to our actual teaching loads in college, admittedly lesser than their teaching loads in K–12. Although most of the comments were simply made as good-natured fun, many of those giving me the jabber did not understand the numerous tasks of a college teacher. We often have large classes, difficult sophisticated labs to prepare, many students to advise, countless recommendations to write, much committee work to do, numerous reports to write, and meetings galore to attend. And in addition, college teachers generally will not receive tenure, which takes five to seven years, just because they are okay in the classroom. They have to be involved in some other professional activity. Some become very active in committee work and college governance. Some become heavily involved in community activities related to their discipline. Some will engage in writing and publishing. Some will write grant proposals. Some will conduct time-consuming research programs. Some work-driven academicians will try to do all of the above. The work of a college professor is definitely not an eight to five Monday through Friday job. I never bothered to explain this situation to the unaware critics. I just ignored them and their aberrant notions about college teachers.

Personally, I always attempted to be active in quality research projects. Research can be so much fun, or so exasperating, so exciting, or so dull, so productive, or so wasting of time. Most importantly, research activity offers one a chance to be truly creative. Well-thought-out experiments carefully conducted can be beautiful in a sense. But the best-laid plans can also go astray. Once a cleaning lady went into the photography darkroom and turned the lights on and, therefore, completely ruined an important experiment that took me two weeks to set up. She didn't read the sign on the door. You just have a good cry!

Once a colleague placed about a hundred plant tissue samples into the freezer instead of the refrigerator following a move from one laboratory to another. These samples constituted an entire two summers of collections that were now absolutely useless because of freezing them. You just have a good cry!

Once someone decided to rid the greenhouse plants of white flies that also congregated on some of my valuable research plants. She had heard that medicinal douche would kill the pesky flies. It did work, but the stuff also killed all of my research plants. At least the plants didn't contract a yeast infection. You just have a good cry!

One time I went around from laboratory to laboratory at a large university where I was temporarily working to see how things were going on the research front. Everyone was swearing about disasters, or dumb mistakes, or colleagues, or experiments that didn't work. I wondered how we, as scientists, ever learned enough information for a textbook to be written and published.

We are all capable of making dumb mistakes. All you need to know about scintillation cocktail is that the chemical is very tough stuff. It can dissolve human tissue in seconds. Dissolving tissue is exactly what this solvent is supposed to do. While working on a research project, I needed to transfer some of this dangerous fluid from a gallon jug into a beaker using an automatic pump device situated on the jug. But I didn't realize that the plastic cap was still on the spout of the pump device. When I pushed down on the pump device the fluid glanced off the plastic cap and squirted directly into both eyes (always the eyes), but two eyes at one time was weird. I quickly turned to a faucet and vigorously threw water into my eyes, but it was already too late. My vision was like looking through smoked glass. And no one was around to get me to an ophthalmologist because it was during a college break. Somehow I got to the ophthalmologist by driving myself without running over any pedestrians, a distance of about four or five miles through the city. I had lost some of the cornea in both eyes, but thankfully my stupid act was not more serious than a few holes in this outer eye tissue. The cornea is one of the fastest growing tissues of the body; therefore, within a couple of days I could see normally again.

During one summer, several of my colleagues had a large grant to conduct research on various aspects of the Mississippi River. They were environmental biologists, and consequently, the project involved various environmental studies. I was a laboratory-type guy. I chased chromosomes. However, bad weather caused my environmental biologist friends to be far behind in their massive project, and they asked me to help. The first venture was a complete disaster. I was working with one of the biologists in a small boat measuring the depth of the water in the river. Very scary black clouds suddenly approached, and both of us thought that it would be a good idea to get off the river. But the anchor became tightly lodged in the rocks at the bottom of the river. I anxiously called out to the environmentalist for his knife so that I could cut the anchor rope allowing us to get out of there to safety. However, he didn't have a knife. We rode out the storm in rolling waves, got completely soaked, and survived to screw up again.

The next time that I went out to solve the mysteries of the

Mississippi River, the day was another total disaster. This time I was working with a different environmental biologist. He bragged about his outboard motor and how it always starts with the first pull. After five or six pulls, I began to worry that the reluctant motor might be a bad omen. Later while out in the middle of the mighty river, extremely high because of many recent rainstorms, the propeller sheared a pin. This situation means that the propeller no longer turns. My coworker didn't have a spare pin. What kind of an environmental biologist wouldn't have a spare propeller pin? The river was extremely fast moving because of the high water. I tried to navigate with the oars, but it became a no-win battle. I thought for sure that we would end up in Dubuque, Iowa, or maybe even New Orleans. When a large raft of nine barges being pushed by a powerful tugboat bore down on us, I somehow mustered enough strength and energy to get out of the way and to get to the shore of a small island. Eventually another boat came by and towed us back to the boat landing.

A mutual understanding was immediately forged. The environmentalists didn't want me to go researching with them anymore (I was bad luck), and I didn't want to go researching with them anymore (they were bad luck).

One summer, an interesting research opportunity with the USDA at the University of Missouri was offered to me. This research entailed microscopic work in a laboratory setting. Driving to Columbia, Missouri, the first summer that I was employed as a plant geneticist brought me through Spring Valley. Four miles south of this town, I was driving past the country golf club, and there in the ditch along the highway was a former teacher friend of mine looking for his golf ball in the knee-high weeds. The next summer, I once again received the USDA appointment to work at the University of Missouri. As I went by the same country club, there once again was the same former teacher friend in the same ditch looking for his golf ball in the knee-high weeds.

Severe weather seems to follow me. I have had so many close

calls while traveling. None were worse than a trip home one weekend from the University of Missouri for my daughter's high school graduation. I left Columbia about midafternoon, and as I approached Iowa going north, the skies turned ugly. By the time I was driving through small towns in northern Iowa, there was no place to seek shelter. Every establishment was closed. Everyone was evidently in basements, and no one was on the highway except one stupid geneticist. The emergency news crackling on the radio indicated that a tornado was on the ground, but it was a bit west of where I was going. As I continued traveling, the radio blared out another emergency that a tornado was on the ground north of me, the direction I was going. A quick look to the sky behind me didn't offer any reason to turn around either. At this point, I was only about twelve miles from the next town across the border in Minnesota (Spring Valley) where my ex-teacher friend lived (the master golfer who played the ditches). So I revved up my Dodge Monaco like I was at NASCAR, making those twelve miles to that town in about eight minutes. The sirens were blaring, and I was the only one still seeking shelter. I found my friend's house, and after answering my frantic pounding on his door, he grabbed a bottle of gin, a bucket of ice, and some glasses and we headed to the lowest level of his house. We proceeded to render ourselves cool, no tornado hit, and at about midnight I finally took off again for home. After some detours because of downed trees, flooding, and other storm damage, I finally got home at about 3:00 a.m.

On still another trip to Columbia, I found myself behind one of those Amish horse-drawn wagons somewhere in Iowa unable to pass it because of a two-lane highway and very hilly terrain. I frequently made an attempt to pass, but always had to pull back into the right lane behind the wagon. Two little Amish boys, probably late grade school age, sat on the back of the wagon facing me. Finally, one of them gave me the obscene finger gesture.

When a researcher at the University of Minnesota called to ask me to join him in summer research, I was elated. As a visiting research professor at the University of Minnesota, I still had to travel to the Saint Paul campus in order to work in their laboratories every week. The time period, however, was in the 1980s during the serious energy crunch. So in a spirit of patriotism, I decided to use public transportation (buses and trains) to get to Saint Paul on Mondays and return home on Fridays. Besides, we only had two cars in the family that were needed by a working wife and four active children who already had driver's licenses.

The first lousy experience occurred on one of the city buses as I was trying to get to the main bus station in Minneapolis. The bus driver was extremely anal. He was screaming at people, and closing the side door toward the back of the bus before passengers could even step off. I had my large, heavy, old-fashioned Samsonite suitcase with me and was ready to depart at my stop when the door began to close in my face too. I yelled some really pertinent obscenities at the driver and used my suitcase as a battering ram to hit the door. The door went crashing open, and as I stepped off the bus, some of the remaining passengers gave me a roaring hand-clapping applause.

Bus stations are something to behold. While waiting for the bus the first week, I was treated to a massive fight in the bus depot. Three guys (maybe four) were fighting over a woman. She didn't seem worth it. I stayed out of the melee. While waiting for the bus the second week, I was treated to view a traveler in the bus depot so drunk that saliva rolled down his chin as he snored away. He had a T-shirt on with the name of a college prominently printed on it. He didn't look like anyone who would go to college. While I was waiting for the bus the third week, I watched a drug raid take place in the bus depot. At first, I thought the cops were blatantly crude picking on a woman holding a baby. However, it turned out that there was no baby in the blanket, just drugs.

The final straw occurred while waiting for a bus on still another occasion. A weaponless security guard was having a serious confrontation with four individuals out where the buses pulled into the terminal.

The odds were very unfair, so I thought that I might be a good citizen and help him out. None of them looked too big or athletic and I was not yet a senior citizen. Then one of them pulled out a gun. I don't know whether it was a real gun or a toy gun. I just got the hell out of there before becoming part of the 10:00 o'clock newscast. That incident finally did it.

After that, I bought a third used car, and my patriotism evaporated. I couldn't take public transit anymore. I decided that busing was for unfortunate people without vehicles and a few drunks.

Living in an apartment during the week while being employed as a visiting professor was not a heck of a lot of bliss either. No one trusted anyone in apartments. People didn't talk to each other. No one even said hello. I wasn't used to that kind of trepidation. When I would come into the apartment building after work, I could hear all of the locks clicking into place as I walked down the hallway. They probably thought that I was a dirty old man. And I could always smell tomato soup as I walked down the hallway. It seemed that everyone ate Campbell's tomato soup every day. Once I tried using a self-laundry place. The one I went to ranked right up there with the bus depot. After that delightful experience, I always saved my dirty clothes until I got home. If I ran out of clean clothes, I would just buy more. And then there was the annual fight over the return of the deposit on the apartment. The landlords always wanted to keep it. I always won the battle, but not without a lot of gnashing of teeth and legal threats.

Because buses, trains, apartments, and laundry places were not my bag, I commuted to the University of Minnesota in the Twin Cities during subsequent summers in order to conduct these research projects. This schedule was more like a trip every other day or every three days with an overnight lodging in a semi-cheap motel or hotel. So now all I had to worry about were those darn tornadoes while traveling. And yes, it happened again. Once on the way home to Winona, I could see this ominous wall cloud ahead of me. But this time I was not going to get caught on the highway. I drove fast into the next nearby town and immediately found shelter in a bar. A bulletin on the television set in the bar confirmed that a tornado was indeed dancing around on the highway. When the sirens began blaring, I asked the bartender where the basement door was located, and he said there wasn't any basement. I had to pick a bar without a basement. So I had another beer. About that time, two excited highway maintenance guys came into the bar with a photograph of the tornado. And indeed, it was rolling along exactly where I wanted to go. This tornado lasted for three beers. I got home late again with beer on my breath, and my wife began to wonder about all those tornado stories.

Tornadoes were not the only weather-related problems. One evening while working at the University of Minnesota, I attended a theater production at the famous Guthrie Theater. Toward the end of the performance, I could hear the rumbling of thunder. It was quite a storm and it rained and rained. Most people, including myself, waited in the hallways and the lobby for the rain to let up. But there was no let up. Gradually, brave souls ran for their cars. I wasn't afraid to get wet, but the constant lightning was of great concern. Hence, I was one of the last persons to dash for the car. The decision to linger was a bad one, because by this time the streets and highways were flooded. This storm unleashed a 10" rainfall to the Twin Cities that evening. I eased my way on to a freeway only to find myself in a long line of stopped cars ahead of me. My quick reaction was to turn off on a nearby ramp. As I approached the viaduct, I could see cars on the low lying freeway submerged in water up to their roofs. Then I ran head on into a rushing river of water. Abandoned vehicles were all over, including a highway patrol car. I gunned the engine to keep the distributor dry and drove very slowly into the raging water coming down the ramp and into the viaduct. At one point, I felt the car beginning to shift with the rushing water, and I prepared to jump. However, the car stabilized, and I slowly danced my way through 18" of water and a myriad of stalled, abandoned cars. Eventually, I reached the motel where I was lodging. I sprawled out on the bed, stared at the ceiling, and mumbled over and over again that I was too old for this out-of-town research stuff.

Still one other weather-related problem had to be battled while engaging in the world of research. I needed to use a very sophisticated instrument called a quantitative interference microscope to obtain some measurements. I couldn't find a laboratory with such an instrument anywhere, probably because they have limited use and cost mega-dollars. I finally located one, unbelievably, in a small forestry laboratory in northern Wisconsin. So on one very chilly day in early February, I journeyed to this lab to make my precious measurements with the rare instrument. That evening, the temperature was -38°. I stayed in a motel that night, and I went out and ran the car for a short while about every two hours. It was reminiscent of my Iron Range days. I filled my own body with some "antifreeze" in the motel bar and emptied my entire suitcase on top of me in the bed in order to stay warm. I got my data, and I survived the twenty-four-hour ice age. This entire ordeal resulted in data for one sentence in one paragraph in one research article that I eventually published. Sometimes such situations become the way of scientific research.

Researching at the "big university" certainly had its rewards. Meeting people from all over the world, interacting with super intelligent people, discovering new information, and getting articles published in major journals are just a few of the many satisfying aspects of doing research. And there was also a ton of laughs along the way. Four of us from our lab decided to have lunch at a famous place in northeast Minneapolis. We had heard that the beef dish was tremendous, and indeed it was. However, the beef and its accompanying sauce were gorged with garlic. Several beers and the garlic orgy made the four of us reek with a strong stench-like odor. Then we hurried back to the university for a seminar by a prominent geneticist. Arriving a bit late, we found no vacant seats in the back of the seminar room where the four of us smelly people belonged, and the moderator beckoned us to sit in some vacant seats in the front of the room. What a catastrophic situation this turned out to be for everyone within olfactory range, including the speaker. I thought that he might collapse at any moment. Even the interior of my car reeked for a month following this misadventure.

During the time that I was researching at the University of Minnesota, I developed a good-sized hernia. Because the University of Minnesota Hospital was close by, I decided to let them make me fit again. The hospital, of course, is also a teaching facility; hence, it seemed like every medical student and intern in the medical building had to look at my battle of the bulge. One female physician came into the room and asked if she could see *it*. I flung open the scanty hospital robe so the good doctor could view *it*. She said, "Wow, *it* is really big." I said, "You damn right." She said, "I mean the hernia." That is what I meant.

Obviously an ideal situation would be to have research grants that permitted me to work in my own labs at Saint Mary's University and eliminate all that travel. Consequently, one has to continually write grant proposals to fund the research year after year. Someone once stated that researchers constantly write grant proposals until either death or retirement intercedes. I was fortunate to have written a number of successful grant proposals to keep my research program active, mostly for researching during the summer months. I had National Science Foundation grants, USDA grants, Environmental Protection Agency (EPA) grants, and various private foundation grants. During my active years, I was awarded a total of thirty-four grants that equaled $1.1 million, money that was used for research, instrumentation, and student work stipends. Writing grant proposals is just another challenge, and some of us enjoyed it because of the competition. You are competing against many others for the money, including the big name research universities. The main criteria are to follow directions perfectly and to put into clear words what is in your head so that it sinks into the heads of the reviewers. Of course, good creative ideas are necessary in the first place.

In one case, an environmental biologist on our staff complained that most of the government grant money was going toward genetic research and very little toward environmental issues. I disputed this notion and further boasted that I could write a grant proposal to one of his environmental agencies and possibly obtain a grant award even though I was a geneticist. The environmentalist called my bluff so I put together a proposal to study the effects of magnetic fields (an environmental connection) on cellular activities (a genetics connection). I sent the proposal to the EPA and received $55,000 to do the work. I didn't really want the grant, because I was already over my head with other research commitments. Now, I had to do the work. During this grant period, I experienced a health problem that necessitated a magnetic resonance imaging (MRI) diagnosis. As the medical people pushed me into the torpedo tube, I asked the attendants whether they knew anything about the effects of massive amounts of magnetism on my bodily cells and tissues. The answer was a somewhat embarrassing "No." I followed up by telling them that I research the interactions of magnetism with cells and tissues. Just before they left me in the tube in order to man the controls, one of them said: "Please don't find any detrimental effects because MRI is a great medical technique." I never did find any major ill effects of low-level magnetism in my research, but I did spend the entire $55,000 trying.

Because I was now doing most of my research in my own laboratories, I had other researchers occasionally coming to Saint Mary's University to use our facilities to accomplish certain aspects of their own research. A researcher at the University of Minnesota (her last name was *Lust*) wanted me to help her use a specialized instrument in our laboratory. I had a lot of experience with its use, and she wanted to capitalize on the information that I might be able to give her. She called me one day and asked whether she could do some work with the instrument on Tuesday about 10:00 a.m. I thought it would be a good idea, and I wrote *Lust* 10:00 a.m. in my appointment book lying on the desk. Shortly thereafter, one of my students came into the office wanting to set up an appointment with me for Tuesday around

10:00 a.m. I pulled the appointment book toward me and pointed out that I was already busy at that time. The student looked at *Lust* 10:00 a.m. and responded: "Yes, I see that you are busy at that time." She added: "You are so organized that you even schedule in lust." I tried to explain, but she was already out the door.

Advising undergraduate students conducting their research projects could be humorous, but sometimes panicky, that is humorous for me and panicky for the students. One group of students found that fruit flies lay many more eggs if they put red wine into their food medium. This finding was important because the students were studying various aspects of egg production and levels of sterility the fruit flies. In fact, the increase of egg production with wine in their diet was almost fourfold, and we actually published the results. I could never figure out why I had to keep buying much more wine than was necessary for these fruit fly experiments. Actually I think I know.

One student was attempting to get corn kernels to develop to maturity on an artificial medium in Petri dishes. The kernels grew nicely, and the results were exciting. When the kernels appeared to be mature, she dissected them. She found the kernels to be completely hollow. Another student was trying to fuse mouse cells with corn cells, and it worked. She immediately ran out and came back with a bottle of Korbel's Brut champagne. We sat on the floor in the lab, out of sight behind the lab tables, and toasted her success. I was pretty sure that this was another stunt that had to be against regulations. Then there was the student doing her research with the use of a flow cytometer. This instrument requires a fluid to flow through a mass of tubes resembling spaghetti. Often times, the lines would plug up, and suction was lost. So after fighting with the machine dozens of times and greatly expanding her vocabulary, she wanted to title her thesis, "A Flow Cytometer That Doesn't Suck Sucks." I vetoed the idea.

Students hated it when their results yielded negative results, that is, something didn't have an effect on something. They always wanted positive results. They wanted things to happen. But such results are not always the way of research. Sometimes I liked negative results, like when one of my student researchers found that my favorite gin was not mutagenic to specialized bacterial cells used in such tests. I had threatened that if she found otherwise, she wouldn't graduate.

My favorite story relates to just such a case of negative results. This student tried to synthesize a unique chromosome rearrangement in the fruit fly, a favorite model organism in genetics. A genetic scheme was devised to possibly make the event happen, and she made all of the appropriate crosses. She then observed over 21,000 fruit flies one by one (called scoring) looking for that one big "bingo." That particular chromosome rearrangement never happened in over 21,000 flies, and the student was kind of despondent about it all. In an effort to keep her from leaping off of the interstate bridge, I indicated to her that it was a great study regardless of the zero for 21,000 results. I pointed out that she did some complex genetics and found out that the events needed for it to happen were too improbable, at least in the 21,000 flies. I also coaxed her into submitting a write-up of her project to a national contest for undergraduate research. Her zero for 21,000 was awarded third place in the national undergraduate research contest, and she received a nice cash award. The moral to the story is that even negative results can be informative, valuable, and worthwhile. Nonetheless this student had enough of counting fruit flies. Today she is a practicing M.D.

I have always felt strongly that teaching and research perfectly complemented each other. In my opinion, research greatly helped my teaching. It put some pizzazz in my class discussions. Firsthand experience could be relayed to the students, rather than regurgitating everything from the textbook. Research allowed me to use and even develop techniques that could carry over to the laboratory exercises that I was teaching. Conducting research immensely helped me in advising students with their undergraduate research projects. Such experience tended to allow me to know what might work and what would not work without the student wasting a lot of time. I vehemently disagreed with teachers at the college level who did not see the benefit of doing research, either as their own projects or as advising student projects. Some of these naysayers would tell me that they wanted to spend all their time on their teaching. I preferred to call their decision a cop-out.

Conducting research benefitted the students in still other ways. Employers liked to see that a student did something in college besides going to class and drinking beer. Graduate schools definitely liked to see that a student did some undergraduate research, even though the research may have been minimal and at a lower level. I observed some students being accepted into graduate schools largely based on their undergraduate research project. And because of conducting research, I had contacts with other researchers at various universities, which certainly didn't hurt in students getting graduate school acceptances. A researcher network does indeed exist out there. I recall giving a presentation to a large audience at a national science conference one time and before I uttered a word, I noticed five of my former students in the audience, all in graduate school or already with Ph.D.s, and all in my academic discipline. How proud I was as I gave the presentation trying very hard to practice everything I preached to them about giving scientific presentations.

The work consisting of mostly full-time teaching loads and concurrently carrying out major research projects in a small university completely consumes one's time. The situation was especially difficult with research that was funded by granting organizations. In such cases, I had to carry out the work, meet the objectives, and bring the project to some kind of fruition. And the granting organization also wanted me to publish the results, which was also time consuming. Combining research with teaching certainly required extraordinary organization and diligence.

Regardless of brutal schedules, travel problems, ominous weather, laboratory mishaps, and a myriad of other difficulties, conducting research gave me a real rush. I was fortunate to be involved in some interesting projects. It was a great feeling to be the first to find something out. The following are a few of the more significant research projects that I have conducted over the years.

In the beginning of my career, I was able to synthesize a two-chromosome double translocation in maize, the first to do so in biological history. This chromosome was abnormal in that it was composed of parts of two normal chromosomes arranged in a very unique way. The two chromosome double translocation was important in gene linkage studies and as one of the methods for increasing partial sterility in certain organisms, that is, for increasing sterility for various purposeful reasons. In subsequent studies, we researched the use of these strange chromosomes as a possible tool to increase sterility in pest insects.

I was also able to research the effects of magnetism on various cellular functions, deemed important by the EPA. A large proportion of the human population is exposed daily to varying amounts of magnetism. People are continually in close proximity to appliances, machines, and motors. Most of these apparatuses function by electricity that moves an armature, which in turn, generates magnetism. After conducting numerous experiments and collecting voluminous data, the results were disappointedly inconclusive. In the first part of the week, an effect could be observed, and later in the week, the very same experiments showed no effect. The experiments were not repeatable. In such cases, a researcher generally deposits the whole undertaking into a large wastebasket. Our data, however, were comparable to that collected by many other researchers conducting similar experiments with magnetism, that is, not repeatable and inconclusive. The jury is still out on this situation.

My biggest research projects were carried out in collaboration with other scientists, mostly colleagues at the University of Minnesota. For a number of years, I studied the molecular and genetic developmental aspects of the storage tissue (endosperm) in maize (corn) kernels. It was a project in which we learned a tremendous amount about how DNA is amplified in the kernel and how that process relates to its development. At least a dozen research articles resulted from this work.

In another collaboration, researchers at the University of Minnesota were able to develop oat plants with one or more maize chromosomes in them. In a spinoff of the project, I, along with several colleagues, conducted a series of experiments to determine whether these concocted oat–maize plants showed an increased photosynthetic efficiency. Indeed the efficiency of photosynthesis was significantly increased. These positive results led to a "eureka" response by all of us on the team (except for running down the street naked).

Another extremely satisfying research project was completed by a team of researchers at the University of Minnesota, Vanderbilt University, Tuskegee University (Alabama), and myself at Saint Mary's University of Minnesota. In this case, we used micromanipulation and nuclear transplantation to place cancerous cells from frogs into normal host tadpoles. Subsequently, we were able to confirm that the cancer cells differentiated into a normal morphology. This result was truly exciting.

Conducting research had many advantages. Foremost was the great benefit to my teaching. I was able to offer my students firsthand knowledge concerning new scientific findings and the employment of contemporary techniques. I am absolutely certain that research made me a better teacher. In addition, the excitement of discovering things not previously reported by anyone else is indescribable. Last but not least, among the many good happenings involved in research is that the work, although grinding and intense, was a lot of fun—most of the time.

Before delving into the world of teaching coupled with research, I used to fish, hunt, golf, bowl, play tennis, go the gym, among other recreational activities. Nonetheless, because of the joys of teaching and the satisfaction of researching and publishing, I have no second thoughts about forsaking most of those recreational activities. And I would do everything the same way again.

My scientific discipline was molecular cytogenetics.
I was fortunate to have access to state-of-the-art microscopy and
instrumentation to carry out my chromosome and DNA studies.
(Courtesy of Saint Mary's University of Minnesota)

Much of my research involved working with the genetic and molecular
aspects of kernel development in maize that also allowed me to do field work,
which was another part of the research that I greatly enjoyed.
(Courtesy of Saint Mary's University of Minnesota)

My undergraduate students and myself, all of whom worked on a large
research project concerning insect control by genetic means. Note the long
hair in the 1970s, including the advising professor.

(Courtesy of Saint Mary's University of Minnesota)

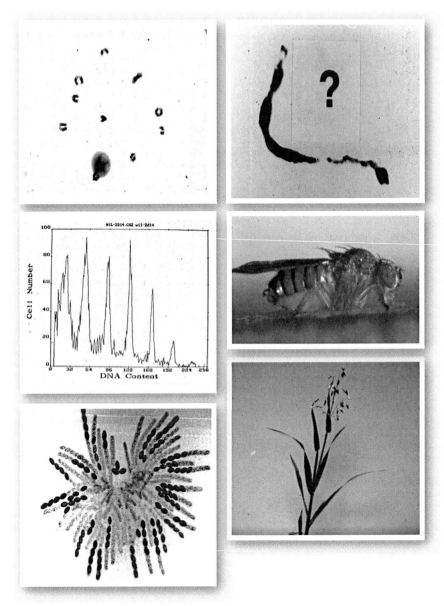

Over the years, I worked with maize chromosomes (upper left), weird
accessory chromosomes known as Bs (upper right), DNA amplification in
maize kernels (middle left), *Drosophila* known as the fruit fly (middle right),
a fungus called *Neurospora* (lower left), and the photosynthesis of oat plants
containing maize chromosomes (lower right).

Chapter 15
Scientists Must Communicate

The noted cell biologist had about fifty highly technical 35 mm slides in his carousel. To begin his talk, he asked for the first slide please. The projector immediately had some kind of an orgasm and quickly shot through all fifty slides in about a minute. Following the last slide, a blank light flashed upon the screen. The biologist, with a straight face, turned to the audience and asked whether there were any questions. Quick thinking and humor are always better than being embarrassed.

Scientists often disseminate their information in the form of oral presentations, poster sessions, written articles, and even authored books. Most scientists understand that they owe it to their profession to publish and give presentations. They feel a responsibility and a need to contribute to their discipline. In most instances, the audience at oral presentations is composed of other scientists or graduate students preparing to be scientists. Occasionally, presentations are also given to the general public. Generally, scientists tend to be much better when speaking to other scientists than with the general public. Those scientists who are adept at giving well-explained presentations to the public deserve a lot of credit. They are talented people. In addition, we are sometimes called upon by the press to give opinions, discuss some big event in the news, or even to explain our own research. Handling these interviews also requires some skill because nonscientist reporters can easily misconstrue what you are telling them. One must strive to make things clear without too much jargon. The task is not always easy, and parts of the story can come out embarrassingly backward in the newspaper.

Due to accomplishing some significant research, I was invited to present seminars at a number of colleges and universities, many of which were major academic institutions. This activity was always a thrill. These opportunities to give talks included the Universities of Minnesota, Wisconsin, Illinois, Ohio State, Purdue, Iowa State, Penn State, LaSalle (Mexico), and Bologna (Italy). Invitations to talk at smaller colleges and universities were just as exciting and included Winona State University, Saint Olaf College, University of Wisconsin (LaCrosse), Augustana College (Sioux Falls), North Dakota State, and the University of Minnesota (Duluth). As a result of these visits, I think that I learned as much from their faculties as they did from my seminars. The people at these institutions were always great hosts, and I benefitted from a lot of free lunches and dinners.

Speaking to large groups of people was never taken lightly. You should be well prepared. You want to be smooth. You do not want to make mistakes. You want to be respected. Probably because of this pressure, I sometimes had dreams about giving important presentations. And these dreams (more like nightmares) were invariably frustrating situations. For example, five minutes to go and I can't find my slides. Or I want to go to my hotel room on the third floor to prepare, and there is no third floor. Or I get lost on the way to the site of the seminar. I always woke up in a sweat. I guess it was indicative of how seriously I took these opportunities to communicate with my fellow scientists.

I seldom gave a seminar without inserting some humor into it. But most importantly, I was almost fanatical about preparing to give seminars at other academic institutions. I would synthesize responses ahead of time to anticipated questions without even knowing what would be asked. I meticulously did my homework. Invariably on the evening before the presentation, I would be in my hotel room studying images by displaying them on the wall of the room with my own projector. I never left home without my projector. Intensive study of the material and the use of many such images made it possible to give a presentation, even long ones, without the use of any notes. In my professional world, using notes was an unwritten no-no and an admission that you didn't know your material well enough. In fact, I would even prepare a brief talk before attending certain events in which I wasn't even on the program, just in case I was asked to say something at the event.

At middle age, I acquired late onset asthma. Besides being concerned about making an ass out of myself, I always feared an asthma attack while I addressed an audience of 200 or 300 people. But asthma attacks never happened. It must have been the emotions churning out adrenalin, which is actually a very good combatant of asthma. Another phobia that I had in these situations was fielding questions from persons who had difficult accents. I have a terribly poor ear for understanding people with accents. I sometimes even have trouble understanding British and Australian people. One time following a talk to a multinational audience, I desperately tried to single out individuals for questions who I knew were U.S. no-accent scientists. The plan backfired. An American scientist from an East Coast university asked me a question in perfect English; however, the scientific sense of the question was so weird that I didn't have the slightest idea of how to respond. Later in the day, I ran into the questioner at the conference, and he apologized for the stupid question. The guy told me that he had his head up his butt. The apology was nice, but I was the one standing in front of 300 people babbling like the village idiot.

One of my first important oral presentations at a conference with a fairly large audience almost induced me to find other work. Another person speaking ahead of me was in the throes of trying to explain some tricky chromosome relationships (called cytogenetics). The poor devil was getting more and more confused by the minute, which, by the way, is easy to do with some cytogenetic topics. A leading cytogeneticist in the country was sitting in the front row. This famous chromosome expert jumped up, went to the stage, took the pointer away from the speaker, and bellowed out something like, "I'll show you what you have here." After explaining the intricacies of the presenter's beloved chromosome, the cytogeneticist sat down again. When I began my presentation, I was fully aware of this cytogenetic assault weapon sitting in the front row. When my very first image flashed on to the screen, the cytogeneticist immediately barked out a question. I barked back something that sounded like an answer (right or wrong) without turning around to face him. My next thought was that if he tried to take the pointer away from me, I might beat him over the head with it. The talk went well and the big guy seemed impressed. Interactions among scientists can be very unpredictable.

Much of my research dealt with plant development; more specifically, I studied the genetic and molecular aspects of how the corn kernel develops. This work is what we call basic research. Such research doesn't necessarily mean that there will be a useful application by next Friday. As researchers, we understand that application may eventually come from basic research, but often times your audience (especially nonscientists) does not realize how science works. I don't know how many times I was asked about whether I was making a better corn plant. The answer was always a blunt no and that I was learning more about a unique mode of DNA replication in the nuclei in the cells of the corn kernel. Usually you would get such questions not long after you had already spelled out this basic research explanation. When individuals in the audience do not pay attention, there is a tremendous urge to be callous. However, I tried not to be that way.

A seminar in Italy proved challenging. Not the seminar itself, but boarding the right train in Florence to travel to Bologna while in Italy was a nightmare. The depot posted many times for the same destination, and I didn't know where in the heck I should be among the many boarding tracks. And the personnel in the information office, full of other bewildered travelers would only tell you to take a number.

Mexico City was another interesting episode. You didn't want the aircraft to land because the city was embedded in a slurry of pollution, easily observed from the air as the aircraft descended. And then there was the drinking-water issue. I drank nothing but beer for six days. Not being able to read Spanish, I only recognized calamari on the menu. So I ate chunks of squid for six days. I really wished that I had learned to read and speak Spanish. The Mexican people, however, were great. They were very friendly, helpful, and appreciative. But they were never on time for anything. For a 7:30 p.m. talk that I was scheduled to deliver, there would be two or three people in the audience at that time. By 8:00 or 8:30, the place would be full of people. Then you begin your presentation. My hosts told me to just get used to the lateness because it was their culture. I never got used to it.

The first of four seminars that I was asked to give dealt with information about writing and obtaining grants. Having had some success in grant writing, I thought that my presentation was full of good ideas, what to do, what not to do, helpful clues, and so forth, all of which would be informative to the audience. However, after the talk and during the subsequent discussion, one of the attendees pointed out that he didn't have any granting sources available for funding of any type, and most of the group agreed with that sentiment. What a waste of a good seminar! Then the next day while giving another talk focusing on my research to a group of graduate students, the discussion was completely diverted to questions concerning life in Minnesota. These students lived in a city overloaded with twenty-some million residents, all trying to get around in constipated traffic on streets that didn't even have painted lines marking the lanes. The traffic situation was like playing bumper cars. I told the students that I commuted less than a mile to work and that I became very angry when I occasionally had to wait for another car at an intersection with a stop sign. I thought these students would fall out of their chairs. I wasn't trying to be an elitist ass. It was the actual truth.

While in Mexico City, I had an excellent opportunity to visit a huge laboratory facility about fifty miles from the city. The complex was a United Nations–funded research facility where scientists from all over the world worked on the development of crop plants for use in third-world countries. I was in a tour group with six or seven Mexican people being shown around by a French scientist.

At one point, the scientist began to explain one of his pet research projects with great zeal. I knew that a former student of mine, now with a USDA laboratory in the United States, was also independently working on that same research problem. Consequently, I was well informed about the nature of this research, and I asked the French scientist if he knew about my former student's work. The guy went ballistic. He screamed at me that he didn't know why this other guy had to work on the research problem because he himself was working on it. I volleyed back that I knew the other guy quite well and he was wondering why you were working on this research problem. I made that part up. The exchange greatly intensified following that comment, and these unaware Mexican visitors didn't know whether they should run, hide, or call for security. We were then transferred to another guide, and things cooled down.

Upon leaving Mexico City, my gracious hosts gave me two cans of smut as a gift to take home. Smut is that awful-looking black and gray fungus that grows on the stalks and ears of corn. As a young-ster, we would never touch it because we were told that it would then grow on our bodies wherever we had touched it. The Mexican people regarded the stuff as a delicacy. Due to their wishes, I gave one can of the "delicacy" to our university president. My can of smut sat in the cupboard for a couple of years. Finally, it was tossed out can and all before someone touched it. The president of our university threw his can of smut out before I left his office.

Our student researchers were also asked to report their research information in the form of oral presentations. Many of them would get very uptight over such an assignment. One student broke out in a rash while she was at the lectern. One other student asked me what she should do if she were to make a mistake during her talk. I told her to simply laugh about it and go on. Well, she made a mistake and began to giggle and giggle and giggle. A twelve-minute talk became an eighteen-minute disaster. She couldn't stop giggling. Another student forgot to use the laser pointer. I got up and handed the laser pointer to her. The student was so nervous that she began pointing to her image on the screen with the laser like it was a stick-type pointer. I asked her to please turn it on.

Students generally didn't mind the actual presentation as much as the question-and-answer period following the talk. They dreaded questions because they had to think on their feet. I convinced one student, who was deathly afraid of questions being asked, that the practice of fielding questions was not a life-changing ordeal. Following her talk, which went reasonably well, the moderator asked if there were any questions, but it was too late. She went out the side door by the lectern and went racing down the hall and out the building.

One of the neat things about working at a college or university, or at least in a college town, is that you get to attend presentations by famous people. To name a few nonscientists, there was Ralph Nader (he answered questions until midnight) and Ellen Goodman (political columnist). Margaret Mead was also very interesting. I found Nobel Prize winner Linus Pauling (famous biochemist) to be a fascinating man. I went to his talk early perchance that I might meet him before his presentation. The chance meeting did happen, and we had a nice conversation. Paul Ehrlich (*The Population Bomb* author among many other publications) wined and dined with a few of us following his talk until after midnight. Communication, regardless of auditorium, hallway, or pub, was always fun and enlightening.

Writing is another way that scientists communicate. Scientists write articles for publication. They desperately try to be exacting and correct. I once published an article in which I asserted that we would probably never be able to clone mammals. Some very strong scientific reasons were apparent to me for making this brash conclusion, and I explained them in the article. A few months later, Dolly, the cloned sheep came along. The Scottish scientists found a way to circumvent the biological obstacle that I thought scientists couldn't circumvent. I should have known better. One should *never* say "never."

Peer scientists referee most articles if they contain scientific information. When scientists author a textbook, the same careful scientific scrutiny takes place. Reviewers, who are always anonymous, can sometimes be a bit vicious. A case in point occurred when I was writing a genetics textbook for nonscience majors. Discussing some of the awful genetic syndromes on one particular page, I wrote that these people with the syndrome were "inept." The reviewer wrote in the margin that "inept" was derogatory and probably not the correct word to use. I certainly agreed with the reviewer, and the word was consequently changed. Lower on the same page, I used the verb "is" when it should have been "are." The same reviewer circled the grammatical error and wrote in the margin, "Now here is an example of being inept."

When the writing of this same textbook was completed (1985, *Genetics, Society, and Decisions*, Charles E. Merrill and Scott Foresman), the publisher's artists went to work. I roughed out what the diagrams should look like, and the professional artists would take it from there. Of course, I would receive their diagrams to review before going to print. Amniocentesis is the technique whereby medical personnel can go into the amniotic fluid surrounding the fetus with a syringe to obtain some of this fluid for genetic analysis. The diagram I received from the artists had the needle of the syringe going directly into the head of the fetus. The artist must have thought the procedure was a vaccination. Even so, why would you carry out a vaccination into the head? This artist needed a lot more biology, or maybe I needed a lot more artistry.

In 2001, I wrote a book titled *Solving Problems in Genetics* (Springer Verlag). The book was a technical treatment of genetics geared for college biology majors. The reason for writing this book was that I always found students in the genetics course having a difficult time with genetic problems. After the book became a reference for my students over several years, I was able to determine with data and statistics that the book definitely increased their ability to handle the dreaded genetic problems. Having already written a book for college nonbiology majors and a book for college biology majors, I decided to write a trade book attempting to explain the basics of genetics to the general public (2010, *The Wonder of Genetics*, Prometheus Books). Most of the publishers that I queried indicated that such a book would not work, that genetics was too incomprehensible and with too much jargon for that readership. But both Prometheus and I were convinced that it could be done.

Another avenue of communication, mostly within your peer group of scientists, is to publish articles concerning your own research endeavors. In this regard, I published eighteen major papers in well-known genetics journals, fourteen other short papers, and twenty-four poster publications shown at genetic and cell biology conferences. Publishing major articles is extremely gratifying because other scientists always review such papers before they get accepted for publication. I always acknowledged the undergraduate students who helped with the actual research and data collections. These young people proved to be capable of doing good research work, and they were very deserving of getting some credit in the article.

An interesting situation seems to exist whereby if something is in print a large proportion of the readers will believe it to be absolutely true. In this regard, I like the true story about a human geneticist at Ohio State University who was confronted by a student in his class over a point that he had made. The student vehemently disagreed with something the professor stated. So the professor told the student to do some searching to see if he could find some more information about the particular topic of contention (an often used ploy by instructors). A day later the student visited the professor's office and pointed out that the professor was indeed right because he had found an article in the library, the content of which completely agreed with the professor's point of view. The professor asked the student who wrote the article. The student hadn't noticed so he retrieved the article from his attaché case to take another look. The professor had written the article. To most people, if it is in print it must be right; however, this assumption is not always so.

Another way to engage in communication, at least with your colleagues and peer group, is to attend scientific conferences. Scientists generally like to attend conferences and symposia. Conferences are meetings where one can listen to experts, learn the newest aspects of the field, interact with others, meet old acquaintances, and, of course, visit new cities. Also, unusual incidents can happen and usually do. For example, your plane might try to land at the Dallas–Fort Worth airport only to be preempted by a tornado going down the runway ahead of you.

Or you might drive to a conference in Albany, New York, and then while you are so close to New York City be naïve enough to drive into the city. Driving into Manhattan on a weekday at high noon is just plain stupid. You have probably seen movies showing the entangled New York traffic. I contend that the real situation is much worse than what you see in the movies. Drivers and pedestrians have no idea what red, yellow, and green mean. There is absolutely no place to park, and waiting for a light to change at an intersection is quite an experience. Swarms of people go across the front of the car, the back of the car, and practically over the car like locusts attacking a cornfield. Light is almost blocked out as if you are experiencing an eclipse of the sun. Getting out of New York City and crossing the George Washington Bridge was like being born again.

While attending meetings in Columbia, Missouri, a man

approached me and asked for some money. I began questioning him about his plight and what he would use the money for and so forth. He related that he was completely broke, couldn't find work, and was very hungry. He also pointed out that he wouldn't use the money for some cheap wine. Maybe I was a sucker, but as we conversed he seemed like a sincere person and really down on his luck. I took him into a fast food place on a nearby corner and bought him a couple of hamburgers, fries, and a soft drink. He practically inhaled the food while I drank a cup of coffee, and then he thanked me. I left feeling quite good even though it was a rather miniscule charitable act. However, shortly after this encounter I learned that a couple of people died due to *E. coli* poisoning from this fast food chain's meals in another state. I began to hope that my small charitable act didn't kill the poor fellow.

As a newly ordained college professor, I thought that I should attend some of the large prestigious conferences. One of the first such conferences that I attended was the International Genetics Conference held in Berkeley, California. The conference was held toward the end of the Vietnam War years, but the anti-war scars were still very prevalent everywhere, especially in the business section of Berkeley. You couldn't find a window anywhere on the famous (or infamous) Telegraph Avenue. All openings to buildings were either bricked in or boarded up. Some intense clashes must have taken place on that street. Hippies still dotted the streets everywhere. I couldn't get into any building where the conference was taking place without my official identification. One time before the speaker said a single word, we all had to leave the auditorium while police searched for a suspected bomb. The bomb scare turned out to be just that—a scare. Why would anyone want to wipe out a thousand geneticists from all over the world? Regard that as a rhetorical question.

After landing at the San Francisco airport, I caught a shuttle to the University of California, Berkeley. The very first person that I met upon stepping off of the shuttle bus asked me, "What are you going to do about it?" My response was, "Do about what?" He pointed out to me in complete seriousness that North America was going to split into two pieces somewhere along the Mississippi River. "And you are obviously one of these scientists, so what are you going to do about it?" In my usual tactful way, I suggested what he might do. Most of the conference participants, including myself, stayed in dormitories on the campus. That very first night, one of the scientists was robbed right in front of the dorm where I was staying, before he could enter the building. The next day, a hippie-like person approached me and tried to sell me something. He told me that this something would send me to heaven for just a few dollars. I told him that I could send him to heaven for free. He moved on. Later that day, three young punks surrounded me on a street corner. As the circle constricted, I thought that a good offense was better than any kind of defense. I swore at them boldly, gave them my Clint Eastwood look, and showed a slight combative stance. They decided to leave, and I thought that I might have to go back to my room to change my underwear. I really had a good time at this conference.

Another conference that I attended in the "early years" was in Washington, D.C. One of the featured speakers was Harvard's E. O. Wilson, a leading authority on sociobiology. Sociobiology is the discipline that considers whether animal behaviors such as aggression, parenthood, cooperation, and selfishness are controlled by genes and play a role in the formation of their social structures. Professor Wilson had written a book on the sociobiology of animals. Some researchers, Wilson included, had registered the possibility that these animal studies might help to synthesize hypotheses explaining human behavior. In other words, they had raised the possibility that some human behavioral traits with a social connection might be inherited such as altruism, generosity, selfishness, hate, love, anger, tenderness, guilt, fear, pride, and ethics. Such ideas had prompted angry responses among both scientists and the general public.

The concept was construed by some people as more genetic determinism. Many people felt that the whole notion was errant and that promoting sociobiology would only serve to justify more social inequities. Some scientists still feel that sociobiology is actually another form of racism, sexism, and elitism. For example, the woman should stay in the kitchen, bare footed, pregnant, holding a kid on one hip while she stirs soup with the other hand, because that is the way she is genetically programmed. Hagar the Horrible (a comic strip) was telling the facts of life to his young son. It went something like the following: Women like to wash, clean, sweep, polish, sew, cook, scrub, shop, and gossip. Men like to play games, tell stories, drink beer, eat rich foods, fight, laugh, and sing songs. It was a comic strip, but the epitome of sociobiology in the minds of some people.

Professor Wilson would have been wise to stop at chapter twenty-six in his famous book, forgetting about chapter twenty-seven. This chapter is the one that brought humans into the realm of sociobiology. Wilson's talk was to be given in a fairly large conference room because sociobiology had become such a controversial topic and a large crowd was expected. Fully aware of this widespread interest, I arrived early for Wilson's talk and still found the room already packed to capacity. It was on this day that I discovered that I didn't have sociobiological genes for being considerate and altruistic. I pushed, squeezed, and elbowed my way to the very front of the room, not far from the speaker's podium. As Professor Wilson began his talk, a vigilante group charged the stage and threw a substantial amount of water on him. I was splashed a little at this historic event. The water-throwing antic was supposed to be symbolic of someone being "all wet." My initial thought was that the selection of genetics as a profession was a great choice. This water-throwing activity was exciting stuff.

I knew Miami Beach would be hot and humid, and I was mentally prepared for it. I was not prepared, however, for all of the other hassles that I encountered on that unforgettable day and night. Upon arriving at the airport for departure in mid-afternoon, I was informed that my flight had been canceled. So the airline agent booked me on another flight to Chicago where I could transfer to Miami, all the while the aircraft sat on the runway waiting for me to board. When I finally boarded, ninety out of ninety people scowled at me. After a three-hour layover in Chicago, I finally boarded a plane to Miami and a shuttle delivered me to the hotel at about 2:30 a.m. I was exhausted, and I had a presentation to give the next morning. I got to *my* room and opened the door with *my* key, and there in *my* room were at least six to eight (I didn't count them) young people of the Cuban nation of both sexes having a great party. These members of both sexes were also very short of clothing. I was absolutely stunned as I stared at them. And they were absolutely stunned as they stared at me. I said something like "Have a good time" as I slowly backed out of the room. After venting a great amount of anger on the hotel clerk, I made him check out the next room he assigned to me. This episode was just another scary incident on the road.

I really felt like an outsider in Miami Beach. It was difficult to find someone who spoke English. Most of the people spoke Spanish. For a quick breakfast, I stopped at a café for coffee and possibly some pastry. The waitress handled the coffee well, but the pastry was completely foreign to her. So I tried other words like continental breakfast, baked things with frosting, rolls, and so forth. She finally brought me some dinner buns. Once more, I felt this tremendous need to learn how to speak Spanish.

Professors are often stereotyped as older, short, pot-bellied people, often bearded, with, of course, eyeglasses hanging over the ends of their noses. My colleague and I didn't fit this mold. We went to a medical genetics conference in Duluth, Minnesota, and at that same time a strike was going on by the dockworkers in the Lake Superior shipping port. Therefore, none of the ships in the harbor could unload their cargo. So what do all of these sailors do to pass the time? They go ashore to Duluth to drink, brawl, and have some fun. So after a couple days of scientific meetings, my colleague and I stopped into a bar for a drink. As soon as we entered the door, the patrons in the bar told us that they didn't want any trouble from us. They thought that we were a couple of pugnacious sailors. We looked at each other and thought that maybe we ought to get out of blue jeans, get a haircut, and comb our hair once in a while. Actually, we felt really pumped up and kind of macho.

This same colleague and I, along with our wives, met at a conference in San Francisco one time. Skipping the meetings for a day, we went up Sonoma Valley and down Napa Valley, stopping at many of the wineries for free wine tasting (all in one day). Thankfully we had a designated driver (my colleague's wife).

I went to an exciting DNA conference in Chicago. The featured speaker was the famous James D. Watson of DNA acclaim. It was a super thrill to briefly meet and hear him in person. After the session, I caught a taxi back to the Chicago train station because I was staying in a hotel located in one of the Chicago suburbs. After I paid the taxi driver, I missed my hind pocket with my billfold, jumped out of the taxi, and went into the train station. At that point, I realized my bad aim with the billfold and the pocket. I had a train ticket and a little change in my pocket that got me back to the hotel, and of course, I canceled all of my credit cards. The next day American Express bailed me out with a new credit card, and the hotel gave me some cash on my credit card. Back at work two days later, I received my wallet in the mail. Of course the money was gone, but all my credit cards, identification cards, and driver's license were intact. I can only surmise that the finder of this wallet looked at my photograph on the library card. It was a photo taken in bad lighting, when I had fairly long hair, and I had a mad police line-up look on my face. I resembled someone out of the Godfather clan. I think the finder thought that it would be a good idea to return the billfold.

One of the annual conferences that I liked to attend as often as I could was the Maize Genetics Conference. The people were friendly, the conference talks were very informative, and the participants liked to party. When I first began to attend this conference, the attendees numbered about 120, mostly males. Many years later, the group of participants was more like 400, with a mixture of males and females. At one meeting while listening to a talk, I counted the number of females in the audience and determined that females made up almost forty percent of the group. This upward surge in women geneticists was really spectacular compared to the early days when Barbara McClintock was one of the very few active plant geneticists.

A number of times, I attended a conference on Valentine's Day, accompanied by my wife. We found that it was very hard to get a last-minute dinner reservation in a nice restaurant on Valentine's Day. Sometimes we would have to call ten or twelve places before connecting. I would plead, fabricate stories, or even pretend to cry. Most of the time we would eventually luck out and get into a nice restaurant. The worst Valentine's Day was when we spent thirteen hours in London's Gatwick Airport because we missed our connection to Florence, Italy. Two or three times that day, we ate cardboard-like pizza and drank cheap wine. It was a terrible Valentine's Day, and my wife kept offering a toast. I think that gesture was sarcasm.

Following a conference in Houston, Texas, I was in the airport waiting for departure. As I stood by one of those small round tables without any available chairs gulping down a hot dog, a guy asked me if he could share the little table. It was a crowded fast food place, and I said, of course he could share it with me. Suddenly he stated in a matter of fact way, "There is more ass in Dallas than in Houston."

I was a bit shocked and didn't quite know how to respond. So I answered, "That is interesting, but how did you come up with this revelation?"

He said, "I just came from Dallas, and there is more ass in Dallas than in Houston."

My weak comical responses and his matter of fact weird assertions went back and forth for a minute or two. Then I noticed a news report on the TV monitor in the fast food place about the massive *ice* storm that occurred the previous night in the Dallas area. I thought

that he was talking about *ass*, but he was actually talking about *ice*.
More proof that my ear relative to accents is very bad.

My wife and I had the benefit of visiting many famous cities while attending
scientific conferences and giving presentations. Here we are enjoying Pisa
and its famous leaning tower.

I am shown presenting a seminar at Winona State University.
At this point in the talk, I was explaining to the audience how large the cell
nuclei were in the developing kernels of maize (quite an exaggeration). Even
as an emeritus professor, I was often sought as a speaker with regard to my
past research and publications.

Chapter 16

Work, Home, and Family:
The Need to Multitask

Fast and furious activities on all fronts made it a challenge to simply keep my sanity and to survive the barrage of activities. I was teaching a full load, some of the classes were large and with accompanying lab sessions, chairing the biology department, carrying on a viable research program, writing grants, working on a book with firm deadlines, advising numerous students both academically and research-wise, being on committees, and attending meetings galore. And I never missed a class because of illness—except once. That once involved a stroke in my fifth vertebra. I thought that it might be reasonable to go to the Mayo Clinic on that particular day rather than conducting my classes.

In addition, my wife and I would try to attend college activities like theater performances, and, in my case, athletics. And we had season tickets to the well-known Guthrie Theater in Minneapolis. But there is more. I also wanted to be a good husband and an involved father to my five children. Consequently, whenever possible we attended our daughter's horse shows, the athletic contests, and the music events in which most of them participated. Also, my wife was employed full-time (sometimes even more), was a coproprietor of an antique shop, was burdened with aging parents three hundred miles away, and still had to find time to be the mother to those five active children.

If the above litany of tasks was not frightening enough, we also purchased and completely renovated a vacant country schoolhouse into a livable home during the height of all these professional and domestic activities. By renovation I mean doing all of the work ourselves except for a new heating system, plumbing, and electrical rewiring.

During the summer before the school year began at Saint Mary's University, we purchased the vacant country schoolhouse. Actually the dwelling was a two-family house when built in 1899 in a beautiful valley about a mile outside of the city of Winona. In 1915, the local school district purchased the house and transformed the inside of the structure into a school for grades one through six. The school served the families and their children in the valley until 1965. At that time, the educational powers in command forced the families in the valley to send their children to the schools in the city (consolidation). From 1965 to 1972, at which time we purchased it, the building was vacant, at least technically. A lot of wildlife found their way into the structure and used it as their home for seven years.

Finding a house during the summer months before actually moving to Winona for the fall school year was a monumental challenge. I was looking for a house that was fairly large, with a big yard, in the country, close to the city, and that was a fixer-upper and not too expensive. Such a find was not very realistic. Then a very old, abandoned, dilapidated country schoolhouse situated in waist high weeds with the right price tag really caught my attention. The interior was a complete wreck, and the place was definitely not livable; but we decided to buy it, move into it, and immediately began living in it.

Okay, how many people have ever purchased a place of residence without their spouse seeing it first? With more than a little trepidation, I called my wife and asked whether we should place earnest money toward a very old, falling-apart country schoolhouse. But I also pointed out that it was a two-family farmhouse at one time before it was a school, and the exterior still looked like a house. She was absolutely elated. After all, it was a *school.* Having spent my entire life in schools since age five, it was the natural thing to do. For my wife, Rose, who had cultivated a strong interest in early American and primitive antiques, it was the natural thing to do. After all, the structure was built in the 1800s (1899). She could hardly wait to see it.

The timing of everything did not permit us to make the place livable before moving into it. Nonetheless we moved into the building because we wanted the children to start school on time. The first half of the year was like camping out. In what would eventually be our kitchen, a lone lightbulb hung from a frayed electrical wire coming out of the ceiling. On the day we moved in, one toilet existed, and it was a mess defying a description. My wife and I drew straws to determine who would clean up the slop pail–looking thing and try to get it to work. I lost. But at least the electricity was on, and the submersion pump in the well was working. Despite this overwhelming situation, our vision for the place immediately began to take shape—at least in our minds.

On the day we moved in, everyone's clothes (all seven of us) were simply placed in a huge pile in the large classroom downstairs. There was no sense in sorting them out yet because closets were not available. Sleeping arrangements upstairs were a bit strange because only two partitioned rooms existed along with one very large room (the other classroom). Only one toilet downstairs was usable following the heroic cleaning efforts by the father of the family. Two days after the big move (Monday morning) was the first day of school. The children were told to find something to wear from the massive pile of clothing in the center of the big room and catch the school bus that would be coming soon. We always assumed that the stressful situation would certainly make our children stronger persons.

One of my very first parental tasks at this point of the renovation adventure was to walk the children around the house and critique the graffiti on the walls. While being vacant for seven years, the abandoned school was obviously a great place for young people in the valley to hang out. Because its condition was in disarray, the building was probably easy to enter. I am assuming that some of them found its confines a sanctuary for smoking cigarettes and possibly other mischievous activities. It was also quite obvious that many of the intruders applied their wit and artistry to the plaster walls. Some of the contributions were innocuous, but others were definitely raunchy. I felt that it was my parental duty to inform the kids which words and drawings were not so bad, and which were really bad (like they didn't already know).

The wildlife, both outside on the property and inside of the house, was abundant, to say the least. We needed to retake the house away from mice, bats, and even squirrels. Snakeskins left behind by molting were found in the basement, and a crawl space under a small part of the house was home to a couple of rats. Southeastern Minnesota is a rich area for wildlife, and our yard was a massive zoo. Small mammals, especially rodents, could be seen daily. However, the exciting observations were the large numbers of deer, wild turkeys, and coyotes that occasionally came rambling through the yard. Deer were as thick as mosquitoes. Most of the time, we would see one to four at a time. Following large tracks in the snow, it was obvious that one ungulate brute came all the way to a dining room window and must of peered in to see what we were doing. And on one occasion, twenty-seven deer all in one herd came out of the woods into the backyard. Some casually came within twenty feet of the back porch. On another occasion, twenty-one deer in one herd descended from the hills into our yard and the nearby property.

Taking back the yard from some of the unwanted varmints was a tremendous challenge, not always met. Warfare with moles in the lawn and mice in the garage were prime examples, which have never ended. Contrary to some reports, deer eat absolutely everything, and they will drive a person crazy unless you eventually accept coexistence. Red squirrels are mean little beasts. Live trapping them and releasing the angry buggers elsewhere worked to some extent; however, some of them seemed to keep finding their way back. Controlling the wildlife is indeed an oxymoron.

Mice getting into the garage was a major problem. The little mammals would make nests everywhere, even under the hood of the tractor. However, it was the last straw when they made nests with straw in the fan area of the heater in the car. They probably found this improbable haven to be cozy and warm. By the way, when you start that heater fan while they are at home in the nest, you make minced mice. Dead mice and their inner parts really stink badly. And cleaning that heater following such an event is absolutely one of the world's worst jobs. So cheese and the simple mousetraps that have been around for decades still work almost flawlessly. Approximately 140 of the mice in our little ecosystem met their demise in the first year of this purge.

The big do-it-yourself project finally began with vigor. We did all of the renovations ourselves except for a new heating system, new plumbing, and rewiring of the house. I thought that working on construction crews during the summer months while in college doing grunt jobs would be helpful to me and it was, but certainly those experiences did not make me a finishing carpenter. The house was in terrible condition so it was a full-scale assault on windows, doors, walls, ceilings, and floors. Openings were closed and closed areas were opened. A walk-up attic (third floor) was envisioned to be a great study/office, and this construction became a successful reality. However, numerous carpentry tasks of the finishing type had to wait until time would permit to give them attention.

Before getting on the do-not-call list, I received a call from a telephone marketer working for a cleaning business. The caller asked about cleaning our carpets. I told him that we didn't have any carpets. He then asked about cleaning our rugs and upholstered furniture. I told him that we didn't have any rugs and upholstered furniture. He then asked about cleaning our floors. I told him that we didn't have floors. The caller asked what we walked on, and I responded "dirt." The bewildered telephone marketer softly said "sorry" and hung up. That was the first time a telephone marketer ever hung up before I did. Of course, I stretched things a little, especially about the dirt floors, but not too much. To some extent, the conversation was indicative of the state of affairs in our dream home.

Soon after transforming the interior of the house into semilivable lodging, attention turned to the exterior of the house. Putting on a new roof, which was extremely steep, with the textured heavier-than-normal shingles and surviving the ordeal two stories up in the atmosphere was something to behold. New porches were added, both front and back, and we finally gave in to hiring real carpenters for the porch jobs. The front porch was reconstructed exactly as the original 1899 house from an old black and white faded photograph obtained from a long-time resident in the valley.

We constructed a patio, driveways, and the sidewalks with pavers and bricks. The city tore up some of the streets that were still made of the old heavy pavers (nine to ten pounds apiece), piled them up on city property, and planned to charge people five cents a paver. When I showed up in my usual parasitizing mood, everyone was just taking them. So I did too.

Next we could move on to the exterior painting parts of the project. The exterior of the house was a drab gray peeling mess. The whole house had to be scraped, and this chore was one very tedious and laborious undertaking. The siding on the house was cedar, and we kept it that way. No vinyl or metal siding for us! We were purists, a type of people rapidly becoming extinct. Some repair needed to be done, and the bare spots were primed, which was most of the house. What color should a country schoolhouse be painted? Red of course!

Any extra help that we came across was accepted with open arms. Some of this generous help actually came from our employer, Saint Mary's University of Minnesota. I was a new professor in the biology department appointed to teach genetics and cell biology courses, and Rose also worked at Saint Mary's University, first in the library and later in the business office. The maintenance department loaned me its dollies for moving heavy stuff, and the biology department allowed me to use its van for picking up materials. The physics shop guy made some implements that I needed, and the environmental biologist tested our well water. Also, a physicist loaned me an instrument to test for radon. Such generosity might sound unusual, but maybe those at the university in charge of things felt sorry for us poor souls moving into a wildlife-ridden unlivable structure. But it may have been because the employer was a small private university. Both the "private" versus "public" and the "small" versus "large" were probably important factors in this unusual show of benevolence. The university seemed genuinely intent on being helpful.

The basement was in horrible condition. Mortar between the rocks in the foundation was falling out, the concrete floor was crumbling everywhere, and monstrous cobwebs hung from all of the joists. In addition, heavy rains brought water into the basement like a sieve. Radon measurements, however, were only slightly above EPA-accepted levels. Abundant amounts of new mortar, an additional four-inch concrete floor, and water proofing the walls took care of both the water and the radon problems.

The finishing touch to the basement was the installation of a wine cellar. Rose found one at an estate sale made of steel racks that could be fastened to the basement wall. It had enough compartments to hold 140 bottles of the fermented grapes, and the temperature of our basement seemed near perfect for our favorite zinfandels, cabernets, and Italian reds. When we picked up the wine cellar unit at the estate sale, the person in charge related to us that she had fifty bottles of French wine (mostly reds and some dating back to the early 1950s).

She was also willing to sell all fifty bottles to us for a total of $100. I have never removed the checkbook from my pocket so fast in all my life. Without trying to be sacrilegious, our basement had transformed from water (rain) to wine.

The building of a huge garage by a geneticist just didn't seem like the right thing to do. But we needed a garage badly, and I was determined to do it. Before starting the construction, a concrete-walled icehouse had to come down, which afforded my first experience with a rented jackhammer. How large should a garage be? Rose and I paced off an uneducated guess and decided on the round numbers of 24' × 36". And heck, because we are going all out, why not make the building two full stories high? And why not build in three dormers on the second-floor gambrel roof? The size of the garage calculated to be 1,728 square feet. It seemed monstrous, but we decided to go for it. Without any architectural plans whatsoever (just some scribbling on a piece of scratch paper), we began building the structure and improvised as we went along. Although building the garage took all of one summer to accomplish, compared to the speed of the Amish doing these things, I still felt that the bearded people could eat their hearts out because of how well the garage turned out.

A great amount of interest by others was shown in our renovation project, probably because of the historical nature of the old building, but also because of the many people who had attended the school. Even some Saint Mary's University students showed an interest in the progression of the project. The awful condition of the house in the beginning stages never prevented us from entertaining, and it never prevented our guests from being interested in what we were doing to the place.

A saying often expressed in the Winona area is that one should buy or build their house on high ground. Through the years, Winona and its immediate area has experienced many floods due to an overflowing Mississippi River. Historically, Gilmore Valley, the site of our house, has also flooded at times. The building of a massive dike eventually kept the Mississippi River in check, but super heavy rainfalls on several occasions still resulted in vast flooding in the region due to the many smaller rivers and creeks that overflowed. On one such occasion, our 10" rain gauge was completely full and overflowing due to a twenty-four-hour steady rainfall (scientific readings were reported as about 15"). The next morning, some of the basement walls in our house were persistently leaking water into our two strategically located sump pumps despite our previous efforts to waterproof the walls. A few minutes after I told Rose that we had nothing to worry about because the sump pumps were working so well, the electric power went down. We didn't have a floor drain in the basement, which actually turned out to be a good thing because such drains were backing up in a lot of homes. Consequently, for about five hours we bailed water with pails from the sump pump pits to the outside of the house in order to keep the basement from flooding. We each manned one sump pump like a his-and-her situation. It was a frantic few hours and an intense workout, but we had to save the wine cellar. And we did save it, along with lesser important things like the furnace, water heater, and water tank.

When one purchases a country schoolhouse that sits in the middle of a large weed patch, at the base of a hill, with a mud flat in the backyard, a plethora of projects other than the structure itself eventually need attention. The list included sidewalks, a driveway, and a patio all constructed with used bricks and antique pavers. An octagon gazebo on the hillside and two small ponds with a fountain and a spray were not a necessity, but we built them anyway. Obviously genes exist for undertaking difficult projects, and we have that DNA.

With the hilliness behind the house and garage, retaining walls were also deemed a necessity. Five fairly large retaining walls and four other smaller ones were eventually constructed to control run-off water and erosion. The retaining walls required a lot of rock, rock native to the local area. We were not interested in the fake-like materials from the big box stores. Such materials would not fit the setting of an 1899 farmhouse and yard. After using the rock from all of our easily available sources on the property, we still needed additional rock. Therefore, on Sunday mornings when most people were in church we would slowly travel the old township roads in the hills and look for rocks in the ditches. Whenever a car came by, we would pretend that we were doing bird observations because it was questionable as to whether our rock pilfering was legal.

Transforming the yard from a hayfield in the front yard and overgrown brush and black locust trees (often thought of as large woody weeds) in the backyard into areas with some aesthetic value was indeed an evolution. Many trees were planted in the open areas, and tangled brush and undesirable black locust in the back were cleared and turned into more lawn that increased the grass-cutting area, which already constituted a weekly monumental task. Flower gardens were also added. Because the building was a school, we inherited hopscotch stones (became a sidewalk) and a bike rack (ended up in one of the flower gardens). Eventually we purchased the 33-½-acre very steep hill and woods adjacent to the back of our lot. This acquisition gave us one heck of a backyard. I later told the seller of the land that we struck oil on it and sent her a photograph with oil wells dotting the hill. It seemed that I wasn't too busy to spend time in the darkroom synthesizing that one superimposed photograph—all for one lame laugh.

From the time of purchasing the deteriorating unlivable country schoolhouse in 1972, events have transpired that tended to reinforce our self-satisfaction of an endeavor brought to fruition. Once midway through the renovation our project was featured in a local newspaper article. The completed renovation has been filmed and presented on a TV program that featured houses of interest in the area. It was one of the houses selected for the Annual Christmas House Tour sponsored by the Winona County Historical Society. And last but not least, one of our sons and his bride were married on the front steps followed by live music on the front porch and a large gala reception in the yard. We have considered all such events as rewarding outcomes.

Everyone needs to occasionally get away from the throes of work. Teachers are certainly no exception. I never seriously felt an onset of burnout. I think that I was always too excited about my work, teaching, research activity, and the renovation of an old country schoolhouse into a home. Besides, as teachers we got all of the holidays off, extended time off at Thanksgiving, Christmas, and Easter. And most teachers, high school and college alike, took the entire summer off to fish or golf. I thought that those who complained about burnout had some kind of a mental problem. But eventually I came to realize that getting away periodically was indeed a good thing. Stress can accumulate when you are responsible for meeting the objectives of your job, helping young people with their missions, and bringing fruition to your grants.

During our time-consuming renovation and all of the professional activities of our jobs, we really wanted to occasionally get away as a family. In addition, we wanted to be good parents and provide our children with opportunities to experience new places. One minor problem (make that a major problem) was that most of our children (80 percent) suffered from carsickness. I swear that they would be sick before we even got out of the driveway. We handled the situation with plastic bags and many stops along the highways. They organically fertilized many roadside ditches. I always maintained that we spent more money on plastic bags than we did on gas whenever we went somewhere.

Regardless of all of the motion sickness, we would go on relatively short jaunts in the Great Midwest region. We took the family to places like the Minnesota Iron Range, the North Shore, historic Galena, Illinois, Amish colonies in Iowa, down the Mississippi River to Mark Twain country, and often to the Twin Cities, mostly to watch Minnesota Twins baseball. On most trips, we enjoyed mixing with the natives. One time, it took us two and a half days to travel back to Winona from Madison, Wisconsin, which is a distance of only 165 miles. We liked to do site-seeing, stop in small towns, use their parks to picnic, play tennis, check out antique places, go to their bakeries, and so forth. After each of these short vacations, we were charged up again to tackle our jobs, research activities, and the ever-present metamorphosis of a country schoolhouse into a home.

Eventually, the children grew out of the ugly vomiting phase. So we chanced a long trip and went off to San Francisco, my wife and I and the three youngest children. We enjoyed getting away, but this trip was besieged with problems. We traveled nonstop in an old Dodge Monaco from Winona, Minnesota, to Reno, Nevada, stopping only for fast food, gas, and human needs. The next day we got caught in the blind spot of a trucker driving an eighteen-wheeler going down a steep mountain highway between Reno and California. The trucker tried to change lanes not realizing we were already in that lane. After side swiping us, we both eventually came to a halt, although it took the trucker and his Sherman tank quite a distance before stopping. The accident knocked off the chrome on the side of our vehicle, bent a fender, and scratched up the left side pretty good. Of course, the semi-truck was undamaged. Our car was still mobile, and the vagabonds from Minnesota continued their trek to San Francisco.

Next, we burned out the brake linings while sightseeing in the hills of San Francisco. Somehow I was able to drive the heap of junk to a garage practically without functional brakes. When we picked up the car a day later, a chrome hubcap was missing (about a $75 loss). The mechanics just shrugged their shoulders. Then on the way back, the speedometer quit working. We had to guess how fast we were going the remainder of the trip. Oh yes, there was one other thing. One lodge in the Yellowstone Park area where we had reservations didn't have any water because of a mutant water pump (completely nonfunctional). No other vacancies were available anywhere. This particular problem meant no water to drink, no shower to take, no Scotch and water for mom and dad, and the toilets had to be primed with a pail of water that I carried from a water hose at a gas station. Yes indeed, this getaway was a memorable adventure.

On another occasion, I must confess that we as the parents of our children were completely void of common sense. We took the entire family fishing on one of those large launches on Leech Lake in northern Minnesota. The guide took us out quite a distance from the home base harbor. At first, the fish were not biting very well. However, when the weather turned ugly, the fish began to bite with a frenzy, so good that we talked the guide into staying out on the lake in spite of the ominous weather. When lightning struck the water extremely near to the launch, we came to our senses and the guide inched the launch back through the heavy rain, wind, and the tall rushes. When we finally got back to the boat landing, we learned that a tornado had passed over Walker, Minnesota, located on the shore of Leech Lake. I pleaded the owner of the launch business not to fire the misguided guide. The stupidity came from the dumb tourists who had to catch a few more fish. Once again, we proved that a lack of common sense could strike anyone at any time.

You never completely get away from acquaintances, either contemporary or previous ones. After teaching hundreds and hundreds of students, you invariably run into them. Sometimes you meet them in airports, usually on conveyer belts going in opposite directions. You run into them in restaurants, concerts, hotels, clinics, and shopping malls. Sometimes you run into them on the streets of faraway cities. Once we were gawking at the weird people on the famous hippie street in Boulder, Colorado. My wife went into a retail shop while I sat on an outside bench. A former female student came along and we hugged (standard procedure). My wife arrived at that time and said that she couldn't leave me alone for a minute and I'm with another woman. Once we were in the Badlands of South Dakota at 6 a.m. It appeared that we were the only visitors at this very early hour. The sun was just coming up on the horizon, and as I looked out at the stunning formations, I thought that I had escaped from the entire world except for my family. All of a sudden, I saw this guy loping across the terrain like an antelope yelling my name. He was another former student.

The young son of a colleague of mine had noticed that his dad and myself were good friends. He asked his dad what does it really mean to be good friends. His dad stumbled around for an answer and finally offered the following explanation. For example, if a good friend has car trouble within 150 miles from home, you would be willing to go pick him or her up. So one night deep into the middle of Iowa on the way home from another one of those mini-vacations in Colorado, our car blew out the alternator. No mechanic was available until the next day. For the heck of it, I called my colleague from the motel that we had checked into and told him about our plight. He asked me where this automotive demise occurred. I told him that I was about 165 miles from home. He hung up.

Before becoming a country schoolhouse, the structure was a two-story family house shown as it looked in 1899. My family and I purchased the structure in 1972 after being vacant for seven years.

In addition to the usual numerous activities regarding work and family heaped upon parents, my wife and I began the metamorphosis of this unlivable country schoolhouse into a livable home. Our family, without outside help, completed most of the renovation, both inside and outside. Top: The photograph shows the house as it was when purchased in 1972. Bottom: The house as it looked after the renovation by my family and myself.

The family, pretending to be architects, carpenters, decorators, and landscapers, also built a two-story garage, established terraced vegetable gardens, formed two small ponds with a fountain and a spray, and planted flower gardens. An octagon gazebo not in view because of the trees was also erected in the backyard. A vacant tumbled-down building sitting in a field of tall weeds and a mud flat in the back was miraculously transformed into a swell home and yard by a bunch of amateurs, all while living in the dust and debris. *(Courtesy of Scenic Concepts, LaCrosse, Wisconsin)*

Chapter 17

Memorable Colleagues: Thumbs Up and Down

When I was a visiting professor at the University of Minnesota, I met a guest scientist from Poland. Whenever foreign scientists came to the university for a visit, everything became so formal. Sometimes when the foreign scientist was introduced to someone, he or she would bow. This was the case with the visiting scientist from Poland. He would bow to each person he was introduced to along the various lab stations. The whole affair was just too darn solemn. When the visitor was introduced to me, I asked him in Polish, "How are you?" The guy broke up. Polish sentences began to run from his mouth like a verbal tsunami, a big smile came across his face, and his arms were flailing away. I told him that he had to ease up. I couldn't go much further in the Polish language than the greeting I gave him. In my mind, I thanked my Polish grandmother for making my day. I had lived with my grandmother for a few years, and she would teach me a little Polish, in addition to the swear words she would occasionally use to describe my antics. I made the day for the surprised guy from Poland.

After fifty-eight years of teaching, one can put together a substantial list of people never to be forgotten for one reason or another. Sometimes it was because they were outstanding educators; sometimes it was because of their unorthodox behavior; and sometimes it was because of our personal or professional differences. Disagreements are easy to come by regardless of whether it is over education, politics, or whatever. For example the elderly head librarian in one of the high schools where I had taught hated John F. Kennedy when he ran for president. She hated me for liking and voting for JFK. I think it was because JFK was Catholic. The day after JFK won the presidential election, a sales representative noticed her in the library angrily shredding the picture of JFK with a letter opener on the cover of a magazine. Now that was one sore loser. I hoped that she paid for defacing the magazine.

When I was teaching on the Minnesota Iron Range, a group of my male colleagues and I would go fishing on the opening fishing weekend every year, usually on beautiful Lake Vermillion in northern Minnesota. We would fish together, eat together, and drink beer together. If someone would raise work topics, he was asked to go home. Later when I changed schools, I helped to organize the same kind of tradition at my new school. We would go to Gull Lake by Brainerd each spring for the fishing opener. We would fish together, eat together, and drink beer together. If someone would raise work topics, he was asked to go home. The big thrill of one of these outings was when a teacher colleague driving the boat decided to motor up onto one of those water ski ramps with the boat. For such insane behavior and other asinine situations, some of these guys became memorable colleagues.

At one of the high schools where I taught, house parties were nearly epidemic. Almost every Friday night after the football or basketball game, one of the teachers would throw a house party. These weekly events were never carried out with much class, just beer (a lot of beer), chips, and various dips. At these particular settings, unlike the fishing trips, school topics would usually be hashed out over and over again. When the party really got going, one of the persons entrusted with the young people of the community would sometimes *eat* a cigarette. This stunt was always abhorrent no matter how much beer was consumed to prepare for it. One of the English teachers really over did it one time and passed out at a particularly long party. Several others took him home by tying him to the fender of a car like a slain deer. That episode was definitely over the line. But Monday through Friday, these fun-loving characters were good teachers and showed professionalism. It must have been something about Friday nights and the opportunity to unwind.

Teachers are probably not any different from those in other professions when it comes to personal relationships. I didn't always see eye to eye with some of my colleagues. During one disagreement in the college ranks, another professor became unglued and screamed at me, "You don't know everything about education," and then stormed out of the room. He was right, of course, but he didn't have to scream such accusations at me. Later that day, we apologized to each other. My apology was for being overly critical about the ways of his teaching, and his apology was for going ballistic about it all. I always thought that we as educators could disagree on educational matters without resorting to yelling and storming out of the room. And I always thought that after heated disagreements we could then go have a beer together. Not always so!

Writing recommendations for your colleagues can sometimes be a very difficult and touchy task. One professor had a very rocky stay at our university, and he received the dreaded nonrenewal notice. He was quite vocal, and at one point during his stay at the university he was served with a grievance. When asked to appear before the appropriate faculty committee, another colleague volunteered to represent him. The guy in trouble asked his representative what he should bring to the meeting and was told to bring a muzzle. When trying to find another position, he asked me to write a recommendation for him. I knew that the guy would have a tough time getting recommendations, so I agreed to do the best I could, considering the circumstances of his departure. Therefore, I thought it would be a good idea for him to see the letter that I had composed. When I showed him the letter that I had written for him, he asked if I would remove this, change that, soften this, and so forth. I calmly made a move to throw the letter into my basket reserved for materials to be shredded and indicated to him that I write my own recommendations for people. He quickly changed his mind and asked me to send the letter unchanged.

Another professor in a similarly awkward position decided to slack up considerably when notified of his nonrenewal. This colleague often pointed out that he was a professor, not a teacher. This assertion really rubbed me the wrong way. He even refused to teach one class that had been assigned to him because it was just an introductory biology course. In my mind, he was blatantly breaking his contract that was still in effect. Then he had the gall to come into my office and ask me for a recommendation. The encounter accelerated until it became one heck of a shouting match. The physics professor in the adjacent office didn't know whether he should just leave, call campus security, or even resort to 911.

Charles Severin, a Christian Brother and a colleague early in my career, was a truly great educator. He had a very dry sense of humor. He did not always think that experts deserved such accolades. Hawthorn trees are extremely difficult to identify to the correct species. A number of species exist in Minnesota, and their characteristics are variable and not well discerned. To prove his point concerning hawthorn trees and experts, he collected seven leaf samples all from the same tree, sent them to the so-called hawthorn expert, and asked for help in classifying the leaf samples. The taxonomic expert categorized the seven samples into four species. Once at a presentation given by a prominent scientist, Brother Charles asked the distinguished speaker a question relating to a statement that was made in his talk about animal cells. The speaker answered the question by saying, "It is an inherent property of the cytoplasm of the cell." To which Brother Charles quickly responded, "I didn't know the answer either."

On another occasion, he was taking a group of students on a field trip up in the bluffs overlooking the university. At one point, a wrong step caused him to fall down the side of the hill. As he tumbled, he grabbed at the vegetation to ultimately stop his descent. Coming to a stop in a sitting position some distance later, he was bleeding and he had a couple of cracked ribs. He immediately looked at a plant that was still in his grasp due to the fall and said, "Gosh, I haven't seen this plant in these parts for years." If a student would answer a question on a Brother Charles exam with a sheer guess that did not make much sense, he would write on the exam, "just words and minus five points." I often heard him say the following when trying to analyze some perplexing biology: "If I ever get to heaven, I have a lot of questions to ask God." I am positive that Brother Charles is in heaven, and I am also sure that he is pestering God every minute of every day.

George Pahl, another Christian Brother, was one of the most unforgettable colleagues of them all. He had a tremendously keen mind, but it worked much faster than his slow-motion mouth. Verbally, he had a difficult time making complete sentences. He continually interrupted himself. Also, he liked to intimidate you by coming close to you, almost nose to nose. An additional circumstance was that he would spew out a mist of his saliva like a spray bottle whenever talking close to a person. So you had a decision to make when you talked with this man: stand your ground and subject yourself to a bath of warm saliva or back away and let him intimidate you. It was a no-win situation. However, Brother George was a very good radiation biologist at one time, and he could write excellent grant proposals. Consequently, he was successful in bringing in tons of money to the university. So partly due to that talent, the Board of Trustees made him president of the university. After all, you want your president to bring in tons of money.

The theater arts department at the university brought in a well-known actor from the famous Guthrie Theater in Minneapolis to spend a couple of days interacting with our theater arts students. When a dignitary was invited to be on campus, a reception was always held for him or her. As a member of the faculty in the theater arts department drove the actor to the reception, he warned the actor that there might be a person present who is a "little off course." The person who he was referring to was a groundskeeper who was always allowed to attend these events. The guy he was talking about was an okay guy, but his elevator simply did not go to the top floor. As the reception progressed, the theater arts faculty member came across the famed actor. The actor mentioned that he did run into the person who had only one oar in the water. The actor further pointed out that he was standing right over there. The faculty member had the embarrassing task of informing the Guthrie actor that the person he was pointing at was the president of the university, Brother George. George Pahl never liked that story, and I couldn't blame him. He was intelligent, a good leader, and an exquisite writer. And he was also filled with compassion and had a heart bigger than any administrator whom I ever worked for. He indeed was another memorable colleague.

I was able to outlast three college presidents. Even in their presence, I would always boast that I would still be around after they were gone. One of them was an excellent speaker. He would have made a great motivational speaker or a coach. Often, he would juice up his talks with some kind of demonstration. At an all-campus convocation to begin the academic year, he was making the point that everyone should have confidence in themselves, that everyone should realize that they are the most important person. So he had several boxes fitted with a mirror on the bottom of the box. He asked several people from the audience, including myself, to look into the magic box and relate the name of the person whom they see. When it was my turn, I said the image looked a lot like Robert Redford. A loud roar of laughter erupted from the crowd. The president hesitated and then said, "Dr. K., you are absolutely impossible." I am sure that not too many people have been accused of being *impossible* in the presence of an entire college student and faculty body. But I think he was right.

Most of my colleagues while teaching in college were fairly discreet in their off-campus actions. One of my less subdued colleagues moved to another university in another state. Being good friends, my wife and I decided to visit his family the following winter at their new location. He gave us some vague directions without a specific address, and we slowly drove down the country road looking for their house as it was described. Then all of a sudden we came across a snow sculpture in the front yard of one of the houses along that road. The sculpture was a big arm and hand in an upright position showing the obscene finger gesture in a very prominent way. That had to be their house. Indeed it was.

Brother Charles Severin was a biology professor at Saint Mary's University of Minnesota for almost his entire professional life. He was a superb botanist and ecologist and a man with wisdom that transcended book learning. Brother Charles was a great colleague and truly a memorable person.
(Courtesy of St. Mary's University of Minnesota)

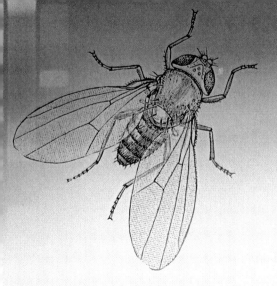

Part IV
PEDAGOGICAL ASPECTS

Chapter 18
Challenges of Teaching Genetics

I used to be a very active outdoors person. I hunted, fished, hiked, camped, boated, and photographed nature. I even knew plant identification almost to the extent of a plant taxonomist, especially the woody plants. I also played tennis, golfed, and bowled. So what placed all of these activities into past tense? I became a geneticist, and the discipline consumed much of my life. Genetics can be an extremely demanding career if you want it to be, and teaching genetics can be a perpetual challenge. The details and language of genetics are often overwhelming for students. Genetics is a specific way of thinking, which is not capable to comprehend by all students. Sometimes "A" students get "D" grades. Sometimes "D" students get "A" grades. Some students study exceptionally hard and still do poorly in genetics. Other students find the subject exceedingly logical with everything falling into place. Teaching genetics tends to be like walking a tightrope between showing empathy for students involved in something very difficult and maintaining reasonable standards.

Genetics, however, was a great career move for me. The discipline is so fascinating, challenging, and fun. Heredity affects everyone's life. We are products of heredity, in addition to our environmental influences. Genetics, the study of heredity, is an extensive component of medicine, agriculture, and biology. It is already becoming a significant part of psychology. Sociology may actually be next.

I found genetics to be an exceptional discipline for pushing students to think, to solve problems, and to make applications, connections, and deductions. In labs, the students had the opportunity to study data and formulate conclusions. One of the biggest deficiencies of college students appeared to be a lack of math ability. Too many students seemed to be almost helpless without a calculator, even for simple arithmetic. Genetics gives the students ample chances to improve their math and statistical abilities, with and without a calculator. In an effort to help students with problem solving (an important part of genetics), I published a book titled *Problem Solving in Genetics* (Springer-Verlag, New York). Using the book as a supplement to their textbook improved the students' problem-solving performance by at least 50 percent, as determined by examination results.

Being a geneticist has brought on some interesting encounters. I sometimes found myself at cocktail parties whereby not everyone was familiar with each other. When asked by people about the work in which I was involved, I always answered that I was a geneticist and a genetics teacher. I had always been irked when college professors would answer such a question as history teacher rather than historian, chemistry teacher rather than chemist, social studies teacher rather than sociologist, and so on. All of these people had earned Ph.D.s and were consequently involved in studying and researching some facet of their discipline, presumably with more detail than anyone else. Almost all of them had at least published their thesis research. Some of them continued to research and publish within their discipline since obtaining their doctorate degrees, in addition to their teaching.

Curious interactions often occurred whenever I pointed out that I am a geneticist, who by the way also teaches genetics courses. The "g" word would sometimes completely quell a conversation. The reaction was almost like I was perceived as being different. I have been at gatherings in which others have slowly, albeit cordially, drifted to other corners of the room when becoming aware of my occupation. No one has ever said that we were doing a good job. I have been at banquets where the conversation around a table of eight or more individuals centered on NFL football throughout the entire evening. When I interrupted and asked in a polite manner whether anyone would like to talk about genetics, I was met with momentary silence, and then the conversation ultimately resumed to NFL football. I don't think that I am paranoid over these situations. Over the years, other geneticists have related similar stories to me about this fear of genetics and geneticists in particular.

I have tried, but without too much interest, to understand this phobia of genetics. It may be that these people were exposed to a genetics class in college, and the results were not good. A few persons have actually admitted such a personal history to me. A good genetics class is not always a walk in the park. In some cases, people associate geneticists with Frankenstein-type activities, that is, geneticists are playing God instead of playing human. Even some faculty members of other disciplines in my own university were extremely wary of what I taught, researched, and wrote.

At least to some extent, I blame television for the lousy perception that some people have of scientists and science. Actual studies of TV programs have shown that 20 percent of the time scientists are portrayed as villainous, 33 percent of the time they fail in whatever they are trying to do, 5 percent of the time they kill someone, and 10 percent of the time they get murdered. These are terrible impressions of scientists and science. Maybe it explains why I sometimes aimlessly wander around alone at cocktail parties. Truly, I have been called Dr. Frankenstein to my face by less timid individuals.

There is no doubt that some geneticists do work on experiments opposed by some segments of the public, like certain forms of genetic engineering. Many people are against genetically modified organisms (GMOs) and other such genetic "advances." I recall attending a presentation in which a noted speaker was discussing various aspects of genetic engineering.

During the discussion following his talk, someone in the audience vehemently declared that it was downright reprehensible to place the genes from one species into a different species. I happened to know that this irate person was taking humulin for his diabetes. Humulin is insulin produced by bacteria due to a human gene inserted into the bacterium. Humans and bacteria are definitely different species. It all depends doesn't it?

On another occasion at a gathering, someone was very upset about my own personal research project with plants in which maize (corn) chromosomes had been placed into oat plants. One question asked of me in no uncertain terms was, Why are scientists constantly meddling with nature? A follow-up question was, Why couldn't scientists leave things the way they were? I happened to know that this person and his wife had attempted to have children several times by the *in vitro* fertilization method. I don't think that *in vitro* fertilization is the way procreation used to be. It all depends doesn't it?

I wrote a trade-type book on genetics aimed at the general public (*The Wonder of Genetics*, Prometheus Books). A serious attempt was made to make this book reader-friendly, at least to the better-educated public. The discussions delved into the many facets of everyday life, some apparent and some not so apparent, that have a genetic connection. Everyday exposure to such genetic connections was described followed with explanations of the underlying genetic concepts in understandable terms. Topics included many of the obvious circumstances such as male–female differences, why individuals are different, chances of having affected children with syndromes, why inbreeding is deemed to be a genetic problem, and controversies surrounding genetically modified foods, stem cells, cloning, and human gene therapy. Other not so obvious genetic connections included sideshows at the circus, women in the Olympics, fountain of youth research, movies, and genetic misconceptions. Although Prometheus Books was very willing to publish a trade book on the topic of genetics, it was surprising to me that many other publishers didn't deem the project feasible. Comments such as "genetics has too much jargon," or "genetics is too incomprehensive" were frequent responses to my queries.

Laboratory exercises associated with a college genetics class, however, generally do not include any controversial or super sophisticated genetic engineering exercises. Students at this level need to learn the basics of the discipline. So they usually conduct straightforward experiments with plant materials, common fungi, and, of course, the fruit fly, which is a genetic mainstay. Genetics and fruit flies have been synonymous for almost the past century. When working with fruit flies, students need to learn how to "isolate virgins" and "clear the bottle." When working with bacteria and fungi, they have to learn how to "streak." Students usually display facetious delight in telling their other classmates what they are doing in genetics. I sometimes visualize a student calling home and telling his or her mother about the coursework in genetics. Last week we cleared a bottle and now we are trying to get virgins. Next week, we are going to do some streaking.

Certain topics in genetics tend to command the undivided attention of the students. As you might expect, sex is one of those topics. Sex and reproduction, of course, form the basis of genetics, so you do need to get into it. Discussions of sexual anomalies always bring an additional raft of questions about topics like the chromosome check previously used in the Women's Olympics, hermaphrodites, and transsexuals. We once had a transsexual person speak to our student body. Becoming a transsexual individual is a voluntary sex change by someone with ambiguous external genitalia or by someone who simply feels more comfortable as the sex opposite to their apparent sex. The reasons are usually psychological, and men who wish to become women tend to choose the sexual change more often than women changing to men. The transformation usually involves both surgery and the application of sex hormones. Our speaker had made such a drastic change. She—I mean he—(I'll just call him/her by R. R.) was a male turned female. The female R. R. had quite a grip when shaking hands with me. R. R. gave a very intelligent and insightful talk about the ordeal of feeling female while being trapped in a male body. R. R. was also a good tennis player, even as a male. My son was also a good tennis player, having played varsity college tennis. R. R. and my son played tennis that evening at the YMCA after her talk until 2:00 a.m. My son has never told me who won, which means I think that I know.

The nature versus nurture (heredity versus environment) controversy was another area that sometimes brought out more than the usual interest from the students. Many of them would have strong feelings in this regard. Such discussions would often lead to the topic of alcoholism, an excellent example of a nature versus nurture controversy. Many of the students had a parent, or an aunt, or an uncle, or a grandparent, or even roommates who were sucked into the demons of alcohol. Most students believed that the condition was at least partially hereditary, which offered me a great opportunity to pontificate on why they should indeed be careful about the use of alcohol. My favorite way to cap the discussions on heredity versus environment issues was to give the students some advice. Should they ever receive a string of "F" grades in their classes, they should ask their parents whether the ugly situation was due to heredity or the environment. Their parents provided both factors.

Evolution was still another topic that piqued student interest, especially the creationism versus evolution controversy. At this point, even the mischievous bad guys in class became saintly. Most students thought that they were Creationists because they believed in a Divine Power; hence, evolution was a bad-sounding word to some of them. But the thinking by these students was basically erroneous. Most true Creationists belong to the fundamental religions, those who believe the words of the Bible exactly as written. Still when I gave a guest presentation one time to a class composed mostly of Catholic students (all nonbiology majors), I could sense their reluctance to accept evolutionary concepts. Later after the instructor of the class surveyed the students concerning my talk, she informed me that the students thought I was a great speaker, but very few of them believed anything that I said. My gosh, changing minds on some issues is very difficult.

People who belong to some of the fundamental religions also tend to be evangelical. They often come to your door to spread the word and to see whether you need to be saved. A woman and her teenage daughter came to my door one time to tell me all about the wrong notions of evolution. I invited them in and respectfully listened to their story. When they got up to leave, I physically blocked the door. I wanted the two individuals to stay so that I could give them the other side of the story. We continued the chat with my controlling the conversation, and they felt very uncomfortable so eventually I had to let them go. I am not sure whether this impulsive act was kidnapping or false imprisonment. That evening as I worked in the front yard, a car full of the saviors drove slowly by my house. I recognized the woman from the afternoon encounter, and she was pointing at my house. I imagined that she was indicating to the others that they should stay away from the evil place.

On another occasion, a middle-aged man came into my yard where I was working in order to relate the "truth" to me. I'm always cordial to these people. They really believe in their evangelical ways. In this case, we got into a nice long conversation. As our interaction progressed, I asked the guy what he did for a living. The man said that he was an accountant for a large construction company. I eventually, and smoothly as possible, worked in another question about whether he ever had to manipulate numbers to satisfy the boss and make things look good for the company. Today I think it is called cooking the books. Surprisingly, the man admitted that he did have to do these deeds on a few occasions, although they were very minor wrong doings. I asked him about the meaning of "truth" and told him to disappear from my property, adding that I would never do what he did.

One often has to teach his or her subject to groups other than those young college students. I once taught a human genetics course to a group of high school biology teachers during a summer session. In a discussion concerning the role of heredity in mentally challenged people, I dwelled on particular data supporting the role of heredity in some mentally challenged conditions. Even if parents have normal IQs, but one of them has a mentally challenged brother or sister, their chance of having a mentally challenged child is greater than the chance for parents with normal IQs who do not have a mentally challenged sibling. A young woman approached me after class with a very disturbed look on her face. She happened to be engaged to a young man who had a mentally challenged brother. I hate when this happens. I really didn't want to destroy anyone's life plans, so I did my best to soften the whole situation by pointing out that the probability was still very low. I switched hats from being the bearer of genetic ill to being cupid. Two or three years later, I ran into this same woman at a teacher's conference in Minneapolis. I just had to find out what had happened to her love life. Alas, she still had not married the guy with the mentally challenged brother. I dropped the conversation without begging any further explanation. My role in this episode bothered me a little, but if you are a geneticist you must act like a geneticist.

I was explaining recombinant DNA procedures and how they led to genetic engineering to another group of high school teachers taking a summer course in human genetics. Following my descriptions of how we can combine the DNA from different species in just about any way desired, I stated, "It is not nice to fool Mother Nature." This statement was part of a popular commercial at that time. I think it had something to do with some butter-like commodity that wasn't really butter. I no sooner got the statement out of my mouth when lightning struck the ground just outside of the lecture hall—and extremely close. What timing! I am sure those twenty-six individuals will never forget the coincidence, especially if they ever fool around with the manipulation of DNA.

For a number of years, I also taught a genetics course to college nonbiology majors. When I first developed this course, very few such courses existed in college curricula, and we seemed to be a charter member in teaching how genetics affects everyone's lives and society in general. Because there was a real lack of textbooks available for such a course at that time, I wrote a textbook titled *Genetics, Society, and Decisions* (Scott Foresmann). The subject matter delved into many societal issues, and the students loved the course. Every topic seemed to be new information, interesting, and even exciting to them. One of my main objectives was to impress upon these students that scientists alone could not, and should not, solve all of the genetic issues that permeate society, that input was necessary from people in other disciplines like theirs, and that there should not be a schism between the so-called "techs" and the "fuzzies." My hope was that these assertions would have an effect upon the students and that it would coax them into becoming active in formulating sound societal decisions and directions.

Many years ago, I was teaching a very basic general education genetics course to members of a large police department in another city, that is, city policemen, state patrol officers, and detectives all working toward the completion of a college degree with the financial help of a big government grant. This proved to be a very interesting experience. They all sat in the classroom located within the police department building with big guns hanging from their belts and radios intermittently going on, and most of them harboring an attitude that aberrant human behavior had no genetic basis whatsoever. A good proportion of them had this deep macho attitude about them, an attitude probably due to their job or even necessary for performing their job. To set the stage for the first exam, I told the group a true story that went as follows. "A few years ago, I was traveling through your fair city, and

I got a ticket for an illegal left turn, whatever the hell an illegal left turn is. Today is the day of reckoning." I then shook the exams in their faces in a sort of rage-like motion. The big macho guys all slumped in their seats. Jeez, how I loved that teaching assignment.

In one incident in the same class with the nice policemen, I was pushing the symbols "A" and "a" around on the blackboard (designating make-believe genes), and someone in plain clothes in the back of the room barked out, "Wait a minute." Because he was in control of the big gun, I waited a minute. His problem was that I was separating gene pairs (same as making sex cells), bringing them back together (same as the act of conception), and generating offspring on the board without any regard to how God fit into the scheme. I eased through the tense moment by explaining that the exercise was just a demonstration dealing with chance and that he could bring God into the equation any way that he wished. A footnote has to be added to the story: A year or so later, I read in a Minneapolis newspaper that this same religious stalwart was arrested for selling confiscated drugs back on the street like an ordinary drug dealer while he was employed in the NARC division of the police department. Consequently, he was given a new home in a prestigious penal institution. Teaching genetics seemed to generate one interesting episode after another.

Here, I am taking a sophisticated pose midway through my long career
at Saint Mary's University of Minnesota. I enjoyed being exceedingly active,
which was demonstrated by a heavy teaching load,
chairing the biology department, researching, writing, and speaking,
often engaging in all of these activities concurrently.
(Courtesy of Saint Mary's University of Minnesota)

Chapter 19
Personal Viewpoints

At the very beginning of presenting the following contentions concerning education, I want it known that I do not pretend to be an expert on the matter. My thoughts on teaching and education in general are only based on personal experiences and my own biases. I don't even know much of the jargon of education. After all these years of teaching, I confess that I don't know the difference between a provost and a vice president for academic affairs, a chancellor and a president, a bachelor of arts and a bachelor of science, an evaluation and an assessment, a goal and an objective, and so forth. I once represented our science division at a curriculum meeting with the professionals at the Minnesota State Educational Department in Saint Paul. After about an hour and a half of verbal bantering with the nice people, I left the building wondering what the hell they had said.

Teaching, along with the entire realm of education, seems very complex to me. What is a good teacher? Defining a good teacher is certainly not easy because good teachers come in many forms. For every thousand teachers, I would guess that there are probably a thousand different philosophies about teaching. When it comes to teaching, I find that some people just have it and some people just don't have it. And teaching success is often independent of intellect, level of imparting discipline, having command of an exceptional vocabulary, and so forth. It seems to me that creativity is a very important component of teaching. And even IQ tests do not do a good job of measuring creativity. I agree with the contention of many others that a distinct difference exists between rote teaching and successfully prompting students to learn.

No matter how long one teaches, the advent of a new class brings on a certain anxiety and excitement. One usually has no idea whether the new group will like the course, whether the students will be astute, and whether they will be responsive and interact with you. A new class is like a crapshoot; nevertheless, you can hardly wait to find out.

I liked to keep the class activities loose and informal. I liked students thinking all the time and volunteering answers to questions in an uninhibited way. Students should be subjected to an educational environment that encourages them to study for the sheer enjoyment of learning, an environment that is permeated with excitement and adventure, and an environment where students can feel free to laugh heartily when appropriate. To foster such an environment, enthusiasm shown by the teacher is an absolute must. But it must be genuine enthusiasm. I liked providing opportunities for students to grow in directions that go beyond blackboards, whiteboards, textbooks, and PowerPoint.

There is a basic list of rules that became very important to me as I attempted to carve out a teaching career. I think being fair to the students was the most important characteristic that a teacher can ever have. Students want to be treated fairly, and they should be treated that way. Along with fairness is being logical and flexible. My adopted attitude was who cares if an assignment was handed in a little later than designated, especially if a good excuse was offered. I wasn't going to read the darn papers until the weekend anyway. Another absolute is to know your subject matter well, I mean extremely well. This part of teaching cannot be emphasized enough. Even the less-endowed students know when a teacher is bluffing or simply relating to a book. And when an occasional information block does strike, there is absolutely nothing wrong with saying, "I don't know—yet." I also thought it was essential to learn students' names as soon as possible. I found the use of humor whenever possible to be of paramount importance; and for gosh sakes, laughing is a good thing.

I have some additional views of teaching. I found it okay to be friendly, but I never forgot that I was their teacher. I liked to teach beyond the textbook, inserting new material when possible. Students generally know how to read. Of course, helping students outside of the classroom was always a must. I enjoyed one-on-one and small-group sessions. I liked to help students wherever and whenever they approached me—in the office, laboratory, hallway, parking lot, washroom, and so forth. I most often scribbled explanations to their questions on scratch paper (used up many trees), and the students would usually take the messy chicken scratches with them.

I always had review sessions with my classes before exams. Even though these sessions were not mandatory, most students would show up for another round of discussions. During these sessions, I would sometimes take the opportunity to teach them how to study. Some students would pose questions online by email, and I always responded to those too. I encouraged my students to study for the sake of learning because it was fun to learn things. I never used unannounced surprise quizzes to goad them into studying. To me, such tactics were just like playing hide-and-seek games.

I hated absenteeism. I never took official role, but just expected everyone to attend class absolutely every day except for serious illness. Especially at the college level, my expectations were based on the notion that college students should show that level of maturity, and that attendance was absolutely necessary to do well in my courses because of the difficult subject matter and my deviation from the textbook. In addition, the parents and/or the students were paying a good amount of money in order to attend classes. I had a motto that I continually related to the students. If you fall down on the way to class and break your leg, crawl the rest of the way. Of course this dictum was not realistic, and there were good reasons to occasionally miss a class. Some excuses, however, were easy to see through, like the death of his third grandfather in one year. One student actually lost her grandfather and grandmother due to a murder/suicide, and she was in class the next day. I wouldn't have been at all upset had she taken a few days off. I thought that I had heard it all until a student showed up late for an exam one morning. He said that he was passing a cattle truck on the way to the university, and one of the passenger cows let go with a major league urination that covered his windshield and nearly caused him to lose control of the car. He said that he had to pull over to a stop, clean the windshield, and compose himself. He did seem a bit shaken when he finally arrived to take the exam. I believed him. One couldn't make something like that up.

Some teachers seem to act like their classes were the only ones the students were taking. I don't think that some teachers realize that the students in their classes were usually taking a full load of coursework, that is, other classes just as important as the class that they are teaching. Also, students have a raft of problems just like their teachers. Many college students have jobs, a love life, difficulties within their family, money problems, health matters, career decisions, and so forth. On top of all those issues, some of them try to find time to engage in athletics and other activities and, therefore, need to miss classes and often try to study in buses and vans because of necessary travel. Some students come out of bad homes, and a few will have to carry on through a parents' divorce. I have observed students becoming very depressed over the divorce of their parents. And through it all, we as teachers are occasionally forced into being amateur counselors and psychologists. One of my students, a college senior at the time, was hard to get along with and a severe pain in the butt to most of his teachers. Upon questioning him about his erratic behavior, he told me that it was because his parents got divorced. So naturally I displayed some sympathy. Then he revealed to me that the divorce took place when he was in the second grade. My sympathy immediately vaporized, and I gave him some stern unsympathetic advice and a kick in the butt.

Most teachers realize that lecturing can be good or bad depending upon how one uses it. Some educators are completely against lecturing. But I think that certain practices can help to make lecturing a good learning experience. Mixing in discussion questions to elicit student responses and engagement will break up a dull monologue. Asking the right question at precisely the right time is like art.

Prompting students to ask questions is just as important. I always tried to find some good in all student questions unless the questions were definitely meant to be stupid and absurd. Some of the worst are "Do we have to know this?" or "Is this important?" and "Will this be on the exam?" In such cases, the students were frankly informed that their question was stupid and absurd. Sometimes getting students to ask questions and become engaged in the topic was extremely difficult. In this regard, classes can greatly vary from each other. On occasion, I have felt that I could walk on my hands naked while kicking popcorn in my mouth without getting a response. Some classes turn out to be just plain dull, and a teacher cannot perform miracles. There is no sense in brooding about it. Showmanship can go too far, but a little of it along with tasteful humor always seems helpful. I have seen student evaluations of my courses in which the students claimed that falling asleep in my classes was absolutely impossible. I have taken such comments as being great compliments.

I felt that it was my job in lectures/discussions to make complex things simple and sometimes to make simple things complex. I relished in getting students to understand concepts, to make connections, and to be challenged. The teaching tools employed included the explanation of things in different ways, the use of visual aids, the use of examples, analogies, comparisons, telling stories, and so forth. Sometimes my examples were actually drawn from movies and cartoons. It is surprising how much genetics can be found embedded in movies and cartoons. I once developed and presented an entire seminar on genetic concepts found in cartoons. I also liked to bring other disciplines into the discussion like chemistry, physics, statistics, and math, which was easy to do when teaching genetics and cell biology. Still other disciplines were sometimes pertinent such as psychology and even sociology. Such teaching strategies made the students realize why it was important to take those other courses. And it was a great feeling when the student would finally understand the concept at hand, a nice thrill for both the teacher and the student.

My thoughts about lecturing straight from the textbook constituted a mortal sin. I rarely even used notes, but when I did they were very rudimentary. Once for the heck of it I taught an entire semester course in genetics without the use of any notes. This was not an easy task considering that my teaching strategy was to ask pertinent questions at just the right time, to bait the students at an exact point of the lecture/discussion, to make specific errors on purpose to see if they were awake and thinking, and to check out their retention with regard to a previous statement in the discussion. This level of preparation, however, should not preclude spontaneity and serendipity in the class. One should always be willing and able to take advantage of such happenings in the classroom. However, how can one accomplish squeezing in these essential parts of the lecture/discussion in a timely opportune manner? Preparation has to begin when the course is initially put together; preparation is continued the day or evening before the class; and preparation is again resorted to just before the class. In other words, it is preparation, then more preparation, and preparation once again.

Science courses with accompanying laboratory sessions lend an added dimension to students' learning experience. Science is really about *doing science*, and laboratory exercises allow for hands-on experience. In addition, I found that the large amount of time spent in the lab was an excellent opportunity to do more critical teaching. It was interesting to note in many cases that some of the "A" students were terrible in carrying out laboratory experiments, while some of the "C" students were excellent experimenters. It was like this latter group of students had brains in their hands. Not to be overlooked as another plus was their writing of lab reports every week. This gave me as their teacher a chance to check out their ability to process data, analyze, and synthesize good conclusions, and also to help them in the manner of writing scientifically.

Setting up and preparing good laboratory exercises is a great amount of work for a teacher. You want the experiment to work in order for the student to obtain useful data. Also, there are safety concerns that need to be addressed in just about every lab session. I am downright elated that after teaching science for so many years, I never had a serious safety mishap of any major consequence. I always devised my own lab exercises and written lab guides using the literature for ideas, tailoring them to fit our own resources, and adding a certain amount of creativity. My main strategy was to design lab exercises to complement the topics being covered in the lecture/discussion part of the course. And almost all lab exercises had to generate data so that students could undergo an analysis of the data and make appropriate conclusions. Even though students had to endure a lot of work in laboratory sessions, some being three hours or more long, and then follow up with a written lab report, it was quite obvious that most students really enjoyed the lab sessions.

When I was in graduate school and serving as a teaching assistant, the head teacher of a genetics course pointed out to his sixty-five students on the first day of class that everyone would get an "A" grade for the course. He further pointed out that because the pressure on grades was now eliminated, they could study genetics for the sole sake of learning. However, he did give them written exams periodically to check on how they were doing. As the teaching assistant, I was also allowed to read the exams. The results were not very good. It is probably true that exams do serve as a motivation to prompt students to study. I witnessed evidence of that notion, at least in this class.

I always gave written exams and based most of the students' final grades on these exams, rather than a lot of reports and term papers (except for lab reports). With written exams, students had to sit directly in front of me as they answered questions with little or no chance to cheat and no chance to plagiarize. I tried hard to make the exams a challenging experience for the student. Over the years, I can use the fingers on one hand to count the number of perfect exams turned in to me. My student evaluations always included some comments about how difficult my exams were, and I took those comments as a compliment. But I graded on a modified curve being a bit tough on the top end of the curve, but quite loose and sympathetic on the bottom end. I really wanted students to earn that "A" grade, but I dripped with compassion on the lower end of the curve. After all, I thought that such sympathetic grading was fair because the exams were difficult. I thought that a difficult exam paired with a sympathetic curve was a way to eliminate boredom for the really good students, without being too lethal for the not so good students.

Contrary to an aversion to making out exams shown by many teachers, I actually enjoyed the task. Putting together an exam was just another chance to be creative. A number of teachers have tried to convince me that multiple-choice questions can be a good way to test students, and that this testing strategy may have its merits, but I never bought into that testing method. And the purchase of ready-made test banks and the use of a machine for the correction of where the student placed little black ovals was completely beyond my style. I liked questions requiring short written answers that asked the students to explain, analyze, compare, connect, show relationships, and unravel dilemmas, and questions like "why" and "how come." Questions that almost completely disallowed guessing. Questions that made the student think. Questions were devised that would force the student to flesh out applications.

After all, if we can't teach students to apply what they have learned in the classroom to other situations, what is the point of going through the motions and then call it teaching? Also the student must communicate with me on such an exam, not just place an "X" or a black oval in a box. And their ability to do well goes beyond memorization although it certainly helps. But *understanding* is the key word here. I can't count all the times when I was in school that I memorized voluminous stuff and got a good grade because of it, when in reality I didn't understand the concept. Throughout all of this educational pontification on my part, however, is the situation whereby one never runs out of questions and problems in subjects like genetics and cell biology. Having that benefit certainly helped me to meet my objectives.

I never used red pens to correct exams because red has the connation of being demeaning. Besides I wrote a lot in the margins of their exams, both positive and negative comments. Hence, the black marker was always my weapon of choice. Some alumni have confided in me that they saved their exams simply because of the notations in the margins of their exams. A timely return of exams to the students was also important to me. Often I found myself reading exams in airports, airplanes, and hotels correcting, commenting, and drawing attention to spelling errors. It requires a lot of time to correct short answer exams as opposed to true and false, multiple-choice, matching, filling in the blanks, and so forth. And one has to have the guts to determine whether an answer is right, wrong, or something in between, especially when a class of thirty students will answer a question in thirty ways. However, there was little indecision with answers like the "Organ of Spices" for the "Origin of Species," or "kotex" instead of "cortex," or firefly genes were inserted into tobacco plants so that they could "light up." I was very happy about students doing well, never gleeful because of wrong answers. I have seen teachers who loved "catching them." My happiness came from situations where the students were doing well on the exams. Then I felt like I was doing my job.

The class was introductory biology composed of mostly freshmen. These young students were awe-stricken, especially early in the academic year. In addition, they were not quite sure what to think of their ranting and raving biology teacher (me). On one particular day, I came into the classroom with a carrousel loaded with 35 mm transparencies. The projector, however, was missing from the room, and this situation was a major problem because my whole discussion was based on the transparencies. The department secretary helped me look for the projector while the students patiently waited in the classroom. Finally, the secretary found the projector in the office of Mr. So and So. As I came back into the classroom with the projector, I screamed to the secretary for all on the first floor to hear that I was going to break Mr. So and So's leg when I saw him. About an hour later, Mr. So and So (an environmental biologist) broke his leg. He was collecting plant specimens for his class, and he accidently stepped into a small hole. The next day Mr. So and So was back in the science building with a big cast on his broken leg. Of course, I had to seize upon the opportunity. At the next class period, I told my trembling freshmen to make note of Mr. So and So and his cast. You do whatever it takes to keep them in line.

Keeping discipline in college classes was several magnitudes easier than in high school. Teaching in high school required a constant vigilance. In college, disciplinary necessities were extremely infrequent. On very rare occasions, I would have to intervene and be a little stern because of some minor problems like not paying attention or talking to their neighbor instead of listening to me. However, I never knew how to properly handle the sleepers in class, even though it was a fairly rare occurrence. Occasionally, no matter how dynamic you think of yourself, someone will head into sleepy land. Sometimes there may have been very good reasons for their slumber. Usually I would gently wake the student and ask him or her to hang in there because class will be over soon. Ridiculing students never worked very well. I once called a student "urea" instead of his real name "Uriah," but that was an unintentional goof. Anyway students should be respected although in the most blatant cases of antisocial behavior a teacher's temperament can really be tested. I confess that I have probably deviated from these pious notions more than once. And respect should go both ways. Although I have never asked that I be addressed as "Mr." in high school or "Dr." in college, I was always addressed that way, even by alumni many years later.

Once in a while the day in the hallowed halls would not be a lot of fun. Some situations are bound to irritate you, even though they are not discipline problems. Students sometimes show up for class with sleep walking tendencies. Students sometimes screw up the best-planned laboratory exercises because they didn't read the directions well. Students sometimes turn in written examinations that you would like to flush down the toilet. Students sometimes display thought processes not commensurate with college. Every once in a while I would spell out to the students, even though I loved pit bulls, that I was going to walk home today and hope that a pit bull would attack me so that I could kill it. Students were at least sharp enough to understand the obvious implication. Things were not going real well, and it might be a good idea to stay clear of the irritated geneticist. At the very least, don't spit into the wind.

Some teachers would hold their class outside on a nice beautiful day. Some teachers would feed their students goodies like cookies, candy, and even pizza. Students can talk some teachers into just about anything. I don't know whether such teachers are just being nice, trying to be popular, or concerned about upcoming student evaluations. I suppose such benevolence is okay to a point, but I never cared about these mushy deviations from traditional education. Call me a closed-minded stiff, but to me a class was a class, a lab was a lab, and a field trip was a field trip.

My biggest concern (even a worrisome thing) about student evaluations was the question about whether the students were challenged in my classes. I liked to challenge students. In cell biology, we derived the enzyme kinetics equations, not just listed them. In introductory genetics, we used probability, not the simple Punnett square. In human genetics, we handled gene linkage using the dreaded maximum likelihood math. In radiation biology, we worked with Poisson distribution, rather than just telling them about it. Most of my student evaluations indicated that they were challenged.

I observed some teachers being deathly afraid of student evaluations. And some of that group of fearful people thought that giving good grades, deserved or not, might correlate with good evaluations. A few studies of which I am aware have shown this correlation not to be true. Nonetheless, I always thought that student feedback was beneficial and that I could learn something from the evaluations every semester. Even after teaching for many years, I could still glean good ideas from students and even adapt. Even old dogs can learn new tricks.

During a career in teaching at any level, one will encounter disturbing situations. My embarrassing moments included not noticing that my zipper in the private area was open, the seat of my pants displayed a large tear, or that water had splashed onto the crouch area when washing my hands just before class. Best thing to do is just to laugh with the students. A severe case of gaseous buildup during class is more difficult to handle. On very rare occasions (thank goodness rare), I excused myself from the class, took care of the "problem," and returned without offering any explanation. I have spontaneously blurted out a curse word or two now and then. Pointing out that the potty mouth incident occurred impulsively and then simply moving on usually averted complaints. A teacher will also have pregnant students in class once in a while. I simply carried on like nothing happened, although something must have happened.

In addition, a teacher is bound to have situations where you have to teach following tragedies. Such experiences in this regard included the Cuban Crisis; the assassinations of John Kennedy, Bobby Kennedy, and Martin Luther King; 9/11; and Katrina. Tragedies can also occur closer to home like a tornado obliterating the home of a student or the loss of four students in an auto accident. I found it best to make a few appropriate comments and carry on with the work at hand rather than overly dwelling upon the ill-fated event. I don't think a patented reaction exists that one can offer to their students in these terrible instances. Everyone must handle it in his or her own way.

Chapter 20

Parting Thoughts

It was a gathering of some alumni of the university held in Des Moines, Iowa. I was asked to address them. It was my job to tell them, once again, how great their college was and how great their college still is. After the short talk, one of my former students, then a podiatrist, came up to me and related how there was one important thing that I had taught him. My first thought was *only one thing?* But this one thing had to be something really stupendous. He pulled out a little notepad from his pocket and showed me how he keeps his daily appointments, tasks to do, and other various notes written in it, just like I always did. This *one thing* completely deflated me—a little booklet. And then there was the student who worked for me as an undergraduate research assistant for a couple of years. Upon her graduation, I found a thank you card on my desk. The note in the card expressed thanks for teaching her how to swear, lie, cheat, coerce, and so forth. I think that the note was in jest, but I am not absolutely sure.

Many serious expressions of thanks were also received over the years. One student became very despondent when as a senior he didn't get accepted into medical school. He had been looking forward to being a doctor (a real doctor) since he was in the third grade, and his applications to medical schools had been rejected. I had him in class during his last semester and soon noticed his increasing absenteeism. I was worried about him, so I obtained his phone number and contacted him. The gist of the conversation (more like an order) on the phone was that he better get his butt in to see me without delay. When he arrived at my office, the main emphasis of my pep talk was that one could surely contribute to society in ways other than being an M.D. And I added that he might even enjoy some other occupation. He resumed attendance in his classes and graduated that spring on schedule. I never had any contact with the student again. About twenty years later, I came out of my classroom, and the former student was waiting for me in the hallway. After our greetings and a brief update, I found that he had obtained a law degree, and he was a circuit judge in the Chicago area. And most importantly he was enjoying the profession immensely. The reason that he was waiting for me in the hallway was to thank me for the great pep talk that I gave to him twenty years earlier. Being a teacher can really have its rewards.

Another student accomplished her undergraduate research project, a biology major requirement at our university, under my supervision. The research required the use of a rather sophisticated instrument called a flow cytometer. This computerized instrument with tubing that resembles spaghetti can often behave badly, which prompts the user to greatly expand his or her vocabulary. Regardless, the student persevered and successfully completed the project and graduated. She was an attractive and talented young woman, and shortly thereafter she won the Miss Minnesota contest at the annual pageant in Austin, Minnesota. My wife and I were at the pageant that evening, because both of us knew her quite well. She had just learned that the Miss Minnesota Award had been given to her, and the stage was the typical mayhem that one would expect. Friends, relatives, and reporters were milling all over the place, and camera strobe lights were flashing away. My wife and I finally made it to the edge of the stage to congratulate her, and she came over to greet us. The first thing she said was, "I heard that the flow cytometer broke down." That machine must have really made an impression on her. My response was, "Forget about the flow cytometer and get ready for Atlantic City; unless of course, you want to do flow cytometry for your talent in the Miss America Pageant."

One of my advisees was a very bright young man, but he had a great knack for getting under the skin of people, including his professors. In spite of his superior academic ability, he was drifting along at barely a "B" average. During his senior year, he told me how he wanted to get into a *top-notch* graduate school and conduct research with a *famous* geneticist or biochemist. So I was compelled to give him a little lecture, actually more like a reprimand for screwing around for three years, and now he was expecting to go on to great heights. I told him that the only chance he had to be noticed by a top-notch school, albeit a slight chance, was to do exceptionally well on the GRE. So he did exceptionally well on the GRE. Then a very well-known biochemist at a prestigious research university called me about the student who was now an applicant to graduate school. I was as frank as possible pointing out that the student was very bright, but that "he needs an occasional kick in the ass" (exact words). The biochemist in his broken English and very German accent said, "I like the bright part. I think that I take him. I like bright." About a year later, I ran into the biochemist at a molecular biology conference in Savannah, Georgia. Of course, I had to ask him about my former student. The biochemist said, "You right. Have to kick in ass." I knew that.

I always hated commencements. I even hated my own graduation ceremonies, the three of the five that I attended. My mother came to my high school graduation; however, not one relative, close or distant, was present at my undergraduate college commencement. This lack of acknowledgement of my accomplishment was much in contrast with what I witnessed in the two colleges where I had taught. Commencement was always a very big deal. Parents, siblings, grandparents, uncles, aunts, and numerous friends would pile into the auditorium for the ceremony. It reminded me of a royal wedding atmosphere, especially at the private university where I completed my teaching career.

I thought the frenzy over commencements was kind of nice, but the actual ceremonies were quite dull. I tried to get the administration to get Woody Allen as the main speaker at a commencement. They ignored my idea. Many people of the graduating class were always blurry-eyed from the previous night's senior activities. The relatives and friends would cheer and shriek uncontrollably when their pride and joys were announced to pick up their diplomas, even though the audience was instructed to contain themselves until the end. A little excitement occurred once when a graduating student released a pigeon in the auditorium during the ceremony. One time, a faculty member fell off the back of the stage onto the floor during the ceremony. That incident really broke the boredom. The guy lived and he also got out of the dull ceremony. I often thought about trying the same thing. All of the commencements were too long. Speakers go on and on saying the same things that have been said at all commencements. On one occasion, an individual from another institution of higher education received some kind of an honorary award at the ceremony, typical of these events. He was supposed to spend only a couple of minutes saying thank you. But no, he had to blabber on and on and on. Finally, I pretended to shoot him with my fingers formed like a gun. The president of our university saw my impulsive gesture, and he slightly nodded his head in approval.

I found that the biggest problem with commencements for me was saying goodbye to the graduating students. You knew some of them for four years, and many of them became friends. I always had a hollow feeling when I went home after commencement. However, they were replaced each year with others. Friendship aside, I hated it when students gave me presents at the close of the academic year.

Even though examinations and grading tasks were over, and the nice gestures could not be construed as bribery, I still hated it. One time I worked my cell biology class unmercifully all semester long. The students were so drained and glad that the end had finally arrived. On the last class day in a very facetious way, I pointed out that even though they loved me, I didn't want any gifts, especially apples and things like that. I ended up with two bottles of good Scotch whiskey. This windfall occurred anonymously and after all of the grading was completed; however, I still didn't like the gesture. Oh sure, I was *really* upset. One student's parents gave me homemade maple syrup for several years running after their daughter had graduated. I hated receiving these gifts so much that I subsequently went to her wedding in Green Bay, Wisconsin, perchance that I might get more maple syrup from the parents. It worked!

It is not a perfect world, and all teachers certainly understand that saying very well. In addition to many of my students who went on to do well in their chosen fields, I had at least four former students who took their lives. I also had one former colleague who committed suicide. As a teacher, you can't help but wonder about these tragic situations. You think about possible signs that were missed. You think about whether there was something different that you could have done. You think about whether they were reaching out, and you didn't know it. You think about the need to be so careful when interacting with students. You think about how amateur we might be when dealing with students and their problems outside of the classroom. And most of all, you hope that you did not contribute to their problem.

The influence that teachers have on students is beyond measureable. It is euphoric when you see students get the jobs that they want, get into graduate schools, get accepted into medical professions, and ultimately accomplish successful careers. I prided myself in being able to identify students who would do well in graduate school. They were not always the "A" students; they were the thinkers and the independent workers, not necessarily those who were great at memorization.

I also bristled with pride when I was able to get a student to quit smoking and to help a student with so-so grades who was dabbling with drugs to ultimately become a Ph.D. molecular biologist. What satisfaction!

Some friendships formed with students have not diminished over the many years since they sat in my classes. And I still get numerous emails from alumni updating me on their domestic lives and careers. My wife and I have attended more than a dozen weddings of former students and a great many class reunions. It is heartwarming to see the large number of students who have gone into careers like my own, that is, teaching and researching in disciplines such as genetics, molecular biology, cell biology, and developmental biology. With regard to my many colleagues, I have been privileged to speak at thirteen of their retirements, which have always been fun events. However, I have had the sad task of giving four eulogies.

What a trip it was to be in academia for so many years. The rewards were overwhelming. I had the opportunity to travel extensively visiting most of the great cities in the United States and Canada and some in Mexico and Italy, and it was a thrill to visit many of the great universities of the world. I met many interesting people including Nobel Prize scientists. Except for commencements and faculty workshops, teaching and research were always exciting and the work really didn't seem like work. After all, I got to interact with bright young minds. For the most part, the students were super great (at least 99 percent of them) making the job easy and fun. Involvement with young people tended to keep myself young at heart. Over those many years, I never experienced stagnation or burnout.

Still not everything was absolutely wonderland. Some of the other tasks that go along with teaching could be tough going, especially being on committees. I was on the faculty promotion and tenure committee for eight years, helping to decide whether people should be able to stay on the faculty or move on. These were difficult decisions, especially in a small university where everyone knows everyone. But it was one of the most important committees in the university, and the faculty has to play a role in its governance. And if we as teachers are truly a profession, we need to evaluate each other. Needless to say there were times when my fellow committee member and I were not the most popular people on campus.

While in graduate school, I received an invitation to play in an alumni versus varsity basketball game at my college alma mater. Although I was no longer a spring chicken, I thought it would be fun to tangle with some good college competition again. Also, I could probably renew some old friendships. On the drive to the college and the game, I bragged to my wife how I was a big wheel on campus and how everyone would probably still remember me. Upon being introduced to begin the basketball game, the announcer butchered my name from "Kowles" to "Knowles." Then I heard a familiar voice among the spectators in the stands blurt out, "Oh yes, a really big wheel on campus."

My name has been a perpetual problem. Almost everyone upon initial contact with me, written or verbal, change my name from "Kowles" to "Knowles." I have had the wrong name placed on a published research article, two book reviews, newspaper articles, radio announcements, organization listings, and most phone calls, except those from my immediate family. The situation has been downright aggravating when one realizes that so many people exist who cannot read, copy, and spell. Asked about what I would change if I could undergo my fifty-eight years of teaching over again, I answered, "my name."

Alas, retirement eventually creeps in for most of us. My retirement speech to the faculty and staff members took the form of the "ten reasons why I was retiring" patterned after the *Dave Letterman Show* on TV. However, my ten reasons for retirement had nothing to do with the job I loved or the students who were so great. Rather it had more to do with mundane things like the cheap wine served at faculty dinners, hard-to-find parking on campus, and being tired of having to train every new president when they enter the university. The talk turned out to be a real hit.

After retiring from full-time teaching in 2008, I was awarded the meritorious Distinguished Emeritus Professor in Biology status and asked to continue teaching on a part-time basis. I jumped at the opportunity to keep a few classes because I still harbored that tremendous need to teach. So I became an adjunct professor for the next four years. The downside was that the office given to me was a small windowless converted storage room. Nonetheless, I didn't care because I was still in the classroom spilling out more "Kowlesism" (a term invented by some of the students). And on the plus side there were no more meetings, committees, academic advising, workshops, and commencements. In fact for a number of years before I actually retired from full-time teaching, I had always refused nominations to serve on committees on the grounds that I was planning to retire soon. That devious ploy (actually a lie) worked perfectly for six or eight years before I actually retired from full-time teaching.

I can point out one more piece of evidence supporting my love for teaching. After teaching full-time at Saint Mary's University of Minnesota for thirty-six years, I could have capitalized on five fully paid sabbatical leaves over those years. I chose to take none of them. Call me crazy, but I didn't want to interrupt my teaching.

One would think that I would have a lot of advice for young, beginning teachers, but I don't. My best advice is not to take too much advice from others. Teachers need to be themselves. But one piece of advice that I have given to beginning teachers on occasion was, "You can't win them all, but you should try." After reaching age sixty-five, the point at which most normal people retire, I was often asked about how long I planned to teach. My answer was always the same, "Until I get it right." Now after fifty-eight years of teaching, I seriously doubt whether it is actually possibly to completely get everything right.

I am shown doing what I love the most—teaching. In this photograph, I am showing a student how to use a flow cytometer, an instrument that can make DNA measurements of hundreds of cells per second.

(Courtesy of Saint Mary's University of Minnesota)

In this photograph, I am explaining the use of an ultra–high-speed centrifuge for separating molecules of different sizes.

(Courtesy of Saint Mary's University of Minnesota)

About the Author

Richard Kowles is Distinguished Professor Emeritus in Biology at Saint Mary's University of Minnesota in Winona, MN. His undergraduate degree was obtained from Winona State University and after completing two masters degrees, one in biology and one in education, he earned a Ph.D. in genetics at the University of Minnesota. He has taught for the past fifty-eight years at various levels, the last forty years as a geneticist and cell biologist at Saint Mary's University. At almost all of the institutions in which the author has taught he has received teaching awards, including the Minnesota Science Teacher of the Year Award in 1984. Kowles is the author of two college textbooks, *Genetics, Society, and Decisions* (Scott, Foresman & Co.) and *Problem Solving in Genetics* (Springer-Verlag). He has also authored a trade book with Prometheus Books geared for the general public titled *The Wonder of Genetics.*